To
MARY
Mother of Sorrows
and
Cause of Our Joy

TREASURES
IN EARTHEN VESSELS:
THE VOWS

A Wholistic Approach

by
Sister Joyce Ridick, S.S.C.
Chicago - Rome

ALBA · HOUSE   NEW · YORK

SOCIETY OF ST. PAUL, 2187 VICTORY BLVD., STATEN ISLAND, NEW YORK 10314

Library of Congress Cataloging in Publication Data

Ridick, Joyce.
   Treasures in earthen vessels, the vows.

   Includes bibliographies.
   1. Vows. 2. Evangelical counsels. 3. Monastic and
religious life. I. Title.
BX2435.R46   1984   248.4'894   84-2817
ISBN 0-8189-0467-4

Designed, printed and bound in the United States of
America by the Fathers and Brothers of the
Society of St. Paul, 2187 Victory Boulevard,
Staten Island, New York 10314, as part of their
communications apostolate.

3 4 5 6 7 8 9 (Current Printing: first digit).

TABLE OF CONTENTS

Poverty

Chastity

Obedience

It is true that the knowledge of one's natural dynamics and structures does not necessarily in and of itself lead to becoming a more spiritual person; what is needed also is the action of grace gratuitously given by God and freely received by a person so that the

> experience of grace is the experience of eternity; it is the experience that the spirit is more than merely a part of the temporal world; the experience that man's meaning is not exhausted by the meaning and the fortune of the world; the experience of the adventure and confidence of taking the plunge, an experience which no longer has any reason which can be demonstrated or which is taken from the success of this world.[8]

Yet, an authentic religious experience is not generally possible where the psyche is turned in on itself, needing to use all its energies to maintain defenses or a natural kind of equilibrium or "status quo." The "earthen vessel" in this case becomes opaque, and the treasures of grace and incarnation may remain hidden or only partially revealed. John of the Cross describes it this way:

> Ah, my Lord and my God, how many go to you looking for their own consolation and glorification and desiring that you grant them favors and gifts, but those wanting to give you pleasure and something at a cost to themselves setting aside their own interests are few.[9]

Religious men and women have, through a particular act of religion—the symbolic profession of their vows—publicly professed to "set aside their own interests," to become an "earthen vessel," transparent to the "treasure" hidden within. Vows presuppose knowledge, judgment, deliberate choice and a free act of the will of the human being which allows the consecrated one to "profess" the evangelical counsels, loving and seeking above all else the God Who took the initiative in loving us (1 Jn 4:10). Therefore, in every concrete circumstance, the religious must seek to develop a life hidden with Christ in God (Col 3:3; Gal 2:20; Perfectae Caritatis). The vows are not a stripping of one's being but an ordering of it in truth, in love:

For when we are stripped of the riches that were not ours and could not possibly endow us with anything but trouble, when we rest even from that good and licit activity of knowing and desiring which still could not give us any possession of our true end and happiness, then we become aware that the whole meaning of our life is a poverty and emptiness which, far from being a defeat, are really the pledge of all the great supernatural gifts of which they are a potency.... *We are like glass cleansed of dust* and grime to receive the sun and vanish into its light.[10]

In this way religious seek to be transformed into what they love, the Lord Jesus, by radical participation in His love, in His will, in His poverty—since the very nature of love itself is to unite and transform us into what we love.

However, as mentioned above, this ideal of becoming transformed into a crystal-clear vessel involves the dialectical interaction between nature and grace. The present work seeks to highlight this dialectic. Each of the vows is considered separately, and concluded with a relevant bibliography. The psychic levels of being, of the human person, of the "vessel" are explicated: a person is a physiological, psycho-social and spiritual-rational being with natural needs as well as ideals or values. The interior struggle to order these levels, and, more precisely, the needs and values at each level are discussed. These levels of being are then related to the "natural" experiences of poverty, chastity and obedience. The transforming experience of grace, the "treasure," makes of the human experience an act of religion, and this is then integrated into a consideration of the experience of poverty, chastity and obedience as "vow."

Therefore, since the religious, as every Christian, is caught in the dialectic of nature and grace, of religious ideal and human need, the vows may become symbols or media of a real, free and authentic "Incarnation" or, on the contrary, they may become symbols of a wounded, disordered human psyche seeking to defend itself. This "becoming" depends not only on the presence of the "treasure" but also on the kind of "earthen vessel." Augustine says that for those given to pursuing the good life, there is also an added danger that when a person imagines he is leading *a good life and doing good,* he may be glorying in himself and not in the Lord.[11] Since self-determination (an ordered self) is necessary for transcendence, for revealing the "treasure," and since self-determination is derived from "correct knowledge of values, the consideration of motives (often hidden) and sometimes from [an understanding of] their possible collision and contradiction in man,"[12] a discernment process is necessary for every Christian. This is particularly true for every religious who professes to witness to the "treasure" in one's "earthen vessel." The religious may be unaware of an underlying unintegrated self, despite the noble proclaimed values of the vows. In this context of the profession of vows, since he/she has no language to express what he *really* is in the depth of his psyche, he may use the language of the "tradition" which surrounds him in religious life—the vows—and thus he may unauthentically appropriate and thereby devaluate, distort, water down and corrupt that symbol of the vows. The words are repeated but the authentic meaning is gone.[13]

Therefore, a part of the consideration of each vow is given to presenting the "ideal," the vow as authentically lived or desired, where the "treasure" of Christ is manifest. Then, in turn, concrete examples are presented of how one may live the vows inauthentically, in one's opaqueness as "vessel," in one's self. The entire work seeks, thus, to indicate the effect that grace may have on nature in terms of transcendence in religious life by facilitating values and ideals—in fact, calling one toward transparency as a vessel. On the other hand, it explicates especially the effect that one's human needs and levels may have on the struggle to become an earthen vessel perfected in its essence—to the degree that the religious may lose his life to find it in the perfection of Christ by referring himself to Him, by transmitting *His* light. Difficulties and regressions on the human levels may make the earthen vessels only that—vessels of earth—unable to be cleaned, perfected, purified so as to reveal more fully the hidden treasure of the vows, the trysting place of the Spouse, the King within. When the treasure of the vows has become for religious an authentic witness to the Incarnation in their lives, the "earthen vessel" of their being has reached perfection in Him—and when an integrated, ordered being, a crystal-clear vessel is prepared, the true light of His love and presence may shine forth more fully, that all may see "only Jesus."

Chicago,
January 1, 1984
The Solemnity of
Mary, Mother of God

Footnotes

1. Romano Guardini, "Realismo Cristiano." *Humanitas,* 1975, 30, 95-101. Guardini indicates that God reveals Himself in Revelation, in people, in things and situations, in happenings.
2. Bernard Lonergan, S.J., "Religious Experience" in *Trinification of the World: A Festschrift in honor of Frederick E. Crowe.* Thomas A. Dunne and Jean-Marie Laporte, Eds. (Toronto: Regis College Press, 1978), pp. 71-83.
3. Cardinal Karol Wojtyla (Pope John Paul II), "The Structure of Self-determination as the Core of the Theory of the Person" in *Tommaso D'Aquino Nel Suo Settimo Centinario. Atti del Congresso Roma-Napoli.* (Naples: Edizione Domenicane Italiane, 1974). See also *The Acting Person.*
4. St. John of the Cross, *The Ascent Of Mount Carmel,* Book II, Chapter 5, No. 6. Cardinal Wojtyla deals further with this symbol in his book *Faith According to St. John of the Cross.* Trans. by Jordan Aumann, O.P., (San Francisco: Ignatius Press, 1981). pp. 50-53 especially.
5. Jacques Maritain, *The Peasant of the Garonne: An Old Layman Questions Himself About the Present Time.* Transl. by Michael Cuddihy and Elizabeth Hughes. (Toronto: Macmillan, 1968), pp. 166-167. See also S. Rossetti, "Psychology and Spirituality: Distinction Without Separation" *Review for Religious* 1981, July-Aug., 507-527.
6. Walter M. Abbott, S.J. (Ed.), *Documents of Vatican II,* (Chicago: Follett Publishing Company, 1966), p. 234. "Gaudium et Spes" no. 36.
7. Examples of depth psychology from a vocation perspective are: L.M. Rulla, S.J., *Depth Psychology and Vocation* (Rome: Gregorian University Press, 1971); L.M. Rulla, S.J., Sr. Joyce Ridick, S.S.C., and F. Imoda, S.J., *Entering and Leaving Vocation: Intrapsychic Dynamics,* (Rome: Gregorian University Press, 1976).
8. Karl Rahner, S.J., "Reflections on the Experience of Grace" *Theological Investigations,* Vol. 3 (New York: Seabury Press, 1974), p. 88.
9. Commented on in John Sullivan (Ed.) *Spiritual Direction.* Carmelite Studies, No. 1. (Washington, D.C.: ICS Publications, 1980), p. 30.
10. Thomas Merton, *Seeds of Contemplation,* p. 169, (italics added).
11. St. Augustine, *Grace and Free Will.* Transl. by Robert P. Russell. (Washington, D.C.: Catholic University of America Press, 1968), *Fathers of the Church Series,* vol. 57, p. 257.
12. Wojtyla, p. 39.
13. Lonergan, pp. 76-77.

ACKNOWLEDGMENTS

I would like to express my heartfelt gratitude to many who have been instrumental in this publication of conferences given to religious. First and foremost, I am grateful to the Sisters in my own Community, the Sisters of St. Casimir, who have supported me, and in a special way to Sister M. Joanella, General Superior and Sister M. Lorenza and Sister M. Adorata, former General Superiors who have encouraged this work even from its early stages. Among my sisters in religion, in a particular way I thank Sister Regina Marie, Sister Karen Spinozzi, Sister Margaret Zalot and Kathleen Yakaitis who, when necessary, typed, suggested, and sustained the pressures of time to help prepare the original conferences. To Sister Julie Shainauskas, who willingly and generously assumed the final work of helping to prepare this book, I am especially grateful.

My very deep thanks to Tim Healy, S.J. who spent considerable time and patient effort in editing the English publication. A special thanks to Rev. Stanley Gaucias for his encouragement, and to Msgr. Michele DiRuberto and Rev. Bart Kiely, S.J. for their invaluable suggestions and insights. Thanks also to Dr. LeRoy Wauck for his timely comments and interest.

To Mr. Pietro Marietti, I am particularly indebted for his noble Christian zeal in first undertaking the publication of this book in Italian and for overseeing its translation into other languages.

Many thanks, too, to Rev. Ciaran McCarthy, M.S.C. and Rev. Michael Kelly, S.J., who assisted in the proofreading of the English-Italian translation.

To my own colleagues at the Institute of Psychology at the

Gregorian University, Rome, Italy—Rev. Luigi Rulla, S.J., Rev. Franco Imoda, S.J., Rev. Bart Kiely, S.J. and Don Giuseppe Versaldi—I owe special thanks for their helpful hints, their support and genuine fraternal interest. To Rev. Jose Esquivel, S.J., of the Greg, I extend heartfelt thanks for his suggestions and very generous collaboration and selfless willingness to oversee the publication of the book for the greater glory of God.

My own family of origin has always been an inspiration and a support in my religious life and values. Profound, heartfelt thanks to my Mom, Dad, Jack and Betty for the roots and the sustenance of my religious vocation and for their love.

To all of these and to all who have been especially close to me in this journey of Faith and Hope and Love, a heartfelt and deep thank you.

I commend to the Lord those who have helped to prepare this work in these ways, and those who will undertake to read it, uniting myself to you only as another "earthen vessel," seeking with you to reveal a gratuitous "treasure" of His love through this common petition:

> Dear Jesus,
>
> HELP me to spread Thy fragrance
>   everywhere.
> FLOOD my soul with Thy spirit and life.
> PENETRATE AND POSSESS my whole being so utterly
>   that all my life may be
>   only a radiance of Thine.
> SHINE through me and be so in me that every soul
>   I come in contact with
>   may feel Thy presence in my soul.
> LET them look up and see
>   no longer me
>   but only
>   JESUS.

(Cardinal Newman)

INTRODUCTION

It is not ourselves we preach, but Christ Jesus as Lord, and ourselves as your servants for Jesus' sake. For God who said, "Let light shine out of darkness" has shone in our hearts, that we in turn might make known the glory of God shining on the face of Christ.

THIS TREASURE WE POSSESS IN EARTHEN VESSELS TO MAKE IT CLEAR THAT ITS SURPASSING POWER COMES FROM GOD AND NOT FROM US. WE ARE AFFLICTED IN EVERY WAY POSSIBLE, BUT WE ARE NOT CRUSHED; FULL OF DOUBTS, WE NEVER DESPAIR. WE ARE PERSECUTED BUT NEVER ABANDONED; WE ARE STRUCK DOWN BUT NEVER DESTROYED. CONTINUALLY WE CARRY ABOUT IN OUR BODIES THE DYING OF JESUS, SO THAT IN OUR BODIES THE LIFE OF JESUS MAY ALSO BE REVEALED. WHILE WE LIVE WE ARE CONSTANTLY BEING DELIVERED TO DEATH FOR JESUS' SAKE, SO THAT THE LIFE OF JESUS MAY BE REVEALED IN OUR MORTAL FLESH.

Death is at work in us, but life in you. We have that spirit of faith of which the Scripture says, "because I believed, I spoke out." We believe and so we speak, knowing that he who raised up the Lord Jesus will raise us up along with Jesus and place both us and you in his presence. Indeed, everything is ordered to your benefit, so that the grace bestowed in abundance may bring greater glory to God because they who give thanks are many.

(2 Cor 4:5-15)

The mystery of the Incarnation is perhaps one of the most consoling yet challenging doctrines of Christianity. It assures us of a real, constant, experiential companionship and presence of God—a real "treasure," as revealed in Christ, and this "treasure" of the manifestation of God is not merely an abstract one. God manifests Himself in the temporal order. He has entered into the reality of this world and our own being, willing to manifest Himself *also* in and through that being and the circumstances of that being. Thus, He truly "dwells among us" in a real, existential manner.

It is, on the other hand, not merely consoling, but also challenging as a mystery. It is challenging because the Incarnation is not a passive, one-time occurrence; it is not a static reality, nor merely only a historical coming of the past. The Incarnation occurs also (but not exclusively) in the dynamism of our present being, a being which is "an earthen vessel." What does His coming into our being as an earthen vessel imply? Where is the challenge?

By nature, we are finite beings: *partially* free, capable of human acts, acts which are the result of an "acting person," the result of self-possession and self-determination through the use of will, reason and enlightened choice. A person is thus able, on the one hand, to master himself, to direct himself to a desired object—in the case of a Christian, toward his final goal: transformation in Christ, to a total response to grace, to the Incarnation in his own life. Thus, being fully human or "perfect" implies some degree of freedom to turn one's energies toward grace and the Infinite, the Absolute One. Yet, on the other hand, the nature of our being is such that we are *partially* unfree: we may choose, and often do choose according to human needs rather than ideals—we choose objects, values, ends which are not in keeping with our "ordered" being as creatures of God, in relation to Him. If St. Augustine says "Virtus est ordo amoris" (virtue is love ordered), we may imply that the challenge of the Incarnation is also the challenge of the very need to "order" our being with its manifold levels so that it may respond more fully to the invitation to "Incarnation" in such a way that, as Paul puts it, "in our bodies the life of Jesus may also be revealed." Only in accepting the reality of things and one's destiny as they are, in accepting ourselves and others as they are in truth, can the "revelatory word of Christ" become clear.[1] When our love becomes disordered, divergencies may occur: rather than glorifying the presence of God, the person glories in himself, putting his hope in himself; rather than being the "agent" of his action, the person becomes subject to these divergencies; rather than preaching Christ Jesus as Lord, the idolatry of self-actualization may prevail; what is symbolically proclaimed as religious experience becomes nothing more than a heightened awareness of oneself due to selective inattentions, to failures in understanding the total truth, and to undetected rationalizations.[2]

The Christian existence—our own being, then—contains the consoling presence of grace, of the "Incarnation" of Christ as "treasure," and the challenging reality of nature as "earthen vessel." It involves the consoling presence of faith and the vitalizing dynamism of reason; the consoling presence of hope and the sustaining medium of memory; the consoling gift of love and the struggling dynamism of the will. There is the transcendent and immanent perspective in the person, as well as an objective and a subjective one. Because of the dialectics of these elements, as Paul puts it, "we may be afflicted but not crushed; full of doubts but not despairing; struck down but never destroyed; dying yet alive in the revelation of Christ in mortal flesh." The Incarnation, then, is a "treasure" in "earthen vessels." Only the person able to master himself can become a gift to others,[3] and a gift to God so complete that he is a clear medium—a vessel so transparent that it allows HIS light to shine through.

The goal of every Christian and, in a particular way, of every religious is to be transformed into Christ by participation with Him; to be so much an existential witness of the Incarnation that the earthen vessel becomes so transparent as to clearly reveal the treasure hidden within. St. John of the Cross uses the famous example of the ray of light passing through a window. The cleaner the window, the greater the amount of sunlight that passes through it, thus communicating its own brightness, its luminous quality and particular characteristics. If the window (or vessel, in our terminology) is totally transparent and clean, the sunlight can be communicated through it to such a degree that the perfectly transparent window will give the exact light as that of the sun's rays and will itself seem to be a ray of light. The window is not essentially transformed into a ray of light—as our nature is not essentially transformed into the Divine, but retains its own nature distinct from the light. It merely "participates" in the ray of light to a high degree. Thus, although it seems to be identical with the ray, the window has a nature distinct from that of the ray itself—but we may say that the window is a ray of light by participation.[4] The conformity of the human will to the Divine Will (incarnation) in love through faith is, in this way, at its peak.

Meditation on the Incarnation requires, then, a focusing on grace as supernatural invitation and presence as well as a focusing on nature as the medium of response and surrender. It requires a consideration of theological-spiritual elements as well as psychological-anthropological ones. While distinctions between faith and reason, grace and nature, spirituality and psychology must be maintained, separation of these is no longer a viable and fruitful, realistic vision of the human person. They may be distinguished, but ultimately need to be united to understand a person in his oneness or totality of functioning.[5]

This present work on the vows is a simple attempt to begin to bridge this dialectic, applying the principles of spirituality and theology to the dynamic elements of psychology of the person. Can this be done authentically? Vatican II has proposed that ". . . if methodical investigation within every branch of learning is carried out in a genuinely scientific manner, and is in accord with moral norms, it never truly conflicts with faith, for earthly matters and the concerns of Faith derive from the same God."[6]

A particular kind of psychology, namely depth psychology, which allows for and in fact centrally integrates the value system of the person,[7] may make an enormous contribution to spirituality and theology, since its aim is to understand the dynamic principles and structures existing in the person so as to be able to help foster the integration of these structures, so that the person may be more available, more receptive to the "treasure" of the Incarnation, the Divine in him, and thus more totally surrendered in love to Him.

TREASURES
IN EARTHEN VESSELS:
THE VOWS

CHAPTER I

POVERTY

"Lord, I am not worthy . . ."

A. Introduction

The New Testament is replete with direct and implied lessons on poverty for the kingdom. The entire passage of the Epiphany Gospel (Mt 2:1-12) in particular has a contemporary dynamism for us as religious: it is a manifest exposition of the experience, the meaning, the value of poverty in Christian love, in the surrender of faith. The Father indicates to us the indispensability of poverty when in His Providence, He ordains the Annunciation to a simple, poor virgin; when He ordains the birth of the Child in helplessness, in an alien habitat, with the barest of necessities and minimal comforts. To the faithless eye, though, God may even seem imprudent and contradictory in the actual events of the Epiphany: royalty leaves its secure comforts to present riches to the "lower caste" with no promise of return, interest or reward. Then, too, the angel's later message to Joseph is not to join the kings to live forever in the fairy-tale bliss of protection and surplus in their palaces, but to continue on in his faithful, creative emptiness with renewed force and vigor.

The Gospel narratives again underline this value of poverty. Christ speaks of the trust of the birds and beasts. He and His followers live frugally from a common purse and minister to the poor. Christ promises blessedness to the poor in spirit, and He encounters and challenges the rich young man. Christ reminds us that the individual who loves his father or mother or family more than Him is not worthy of discipleship. Finally, the ultimate self-abandonment of Christ on the cross speaks of the essential importance of poverty.

In the scriptural invitation to poverty, we see that God proposes a way of life which remedies the old concupiscence to greed. He reminds us that in order to follow him, we must leave all things to live a contemplative life in action. We must do this by developing the image of Christ in ourselves through a humble acceptance of our need of salvation because of our finiteness—our nearness to death, the limitations and tentativeness of our insights and capacities. Therefore, for *all* Christians, living according to the Gospels necessarily implies poverty.

Moreover, if we study the integral character of the consecration of the Christian to Christ in faith, hope and love within the structure of religious life, we find the counsel of poverty prominent among its elements. Religious life finds the embodiment of faith, hope and love in the "flesh" of radical poverty "voluntarily embraced in imitation of Christ."[1] Theologically, it is a consecration of the body and of possessions as vehicles of our presence to God as well as of our presence in and to the world. It is a "share in the poverty of Christ, who became poor for our sake when, before, he had been rich, that we might be enriched by his poverty" (2 Cor 8:9; cf. Mt 8:20). If we seek, then, to be authentic religious, the counsel of poverty is indispensable. What, then, is this counsel of poverty?

B. Defining the Concepts of the Counsel of Poverty: The Ideals

The counsel of poverty can be defined in two ways: by specifying what it is *not* and what it *is*.

First of all, poverty is *not* a concept, or a law, or a thing, or a substance which can be analyzed, dissected or put through a filter to separate cultural and psychological elements from the pure

Gospel essence.[2] Poverty, Ladislas Orsy tells us, is an intangible gift: an *attitude* which grows out of a relationship between two persons who love each other. It is initiated by God through the gift of Himself to us.[3] To accept this gift means that we allow ourselves to be led by Him. When there is great love between God and us, our relation to the material world is transformed: some objects, some levels of our being, while remaining vital and necessary, decrease in importance; others become rich in meaning.

With the acknowledgment of God's personal love in our hearts and His action in our lives, comes the awareness of our belongingness to Christ. There comes about a change of heart, of attitude. We become aware that Someone has entered our lives. The hard core of our self-centeredness has been pierced. We agree to open our hearts to the love of God, to surrender. We are willing to accept all the joy and pain that are entailed in change, in loving Christ on a deeper level than we had previously.

Thus, poverty should be a witness to our interior values: the faith, hope and love we have in Christ. It should reveal our surrendered, dedicated trust in Him. Poverty becomes an *interior attitude*, springing from a deep value of which the vow is only a sign. Seen in this way, poverty is not merely a behavior or a mere concern with things—but rather is a concern with a Being, a Person. It is an attitude which becomes a condition, a situation, a complex of attitudes, and a dimension of an integrated life within and between both persons and communities. It is an attitude embodied in a vowed way of life which becomes an exterior symbol of the interior surrender. Father Thomas Clarke calls it a creative symbol of the kind of commitment we have made to God and to each other: a distinctive way of being with God and with one's fellow man.[4]

It follows, then, that poverty is *not* a deprivation of material goods, or possessions, persons or social interactions. It *is* an integration, a liberation and a revelation. It is a realization of the givenness of all things—that is, an acute awareness of all God has given us at our own core levels. It is a way of giving our finiteness to the Giver of all good things so as to be completed and transformed in Him. Thus, poverty is an expression of the integration

of our being: an ordering of things and people according to the
essential significance within them and within ourselves. Poverty
becomes an expression of the transcendent, self-forgetful love
proposed by God.

Poverty for Christ and the Kingdom, seen in this way, is a
liberation. It is organizing and integrative; it is a freedom from
excessive preoccupation with food, clothing, shelter and particular persons. It is availability as well as radical detachment in its
broadest sense. The fact that we no longer belong to ourselves
(i.e., this dispossession of ourselves) implies a rooting *out* of our
possessiveness on all levels and at the same time a rootedness in
Christ. Poverty becomes freedom for the consolidation of a way
which most manifests our belonging to Christ. Our exterior dispossession, therefore, expresses a fundamental inspiration, a
positive interior detachment from self.

Clearly then, poverty in its ultimate understanding is not
deprivation, but a directing of the levels of our being, a distancing
from fixation on any one level, so as to be free to reach and possess
a total integrated intimacy with Christ through all of them. Self-
abandonment is surrender, not deprivation—because through it
is found the poorness of being truly human *and* the richness
which Christ possessed through intimacy with the Father.

Thirdly, because it is not a way or a deprivation, but an
underlying universal attitude, poverty is not necessarily expressed
in externals by a totally uniform way of life. Ignatius was neither
Benedict nor Francis. Fr. Clarke says:

> judgment regarding this or that dimension of our poverty,
> the measure of material frugality, the measure of autonomy
> given to individuals or to local groups, the matter of fixed
> income, and so forth will take place not so much by fixed
> principles or with reference to a fixed center, as by *discern-
> ment of congruity*, always with reference to the whole of life of
> the individual . . . or of a community.[5]

The interior attitude is one of personal abandonment and its
exterior expression must be congruous to it, though the expression may be multiple in form.[6] There is no "perfect" way of

poverty since it is a means and not an end in itself. No true lover feels complacent about the external expression of his love. Even when a person has given all, it is nothing, it is inadequate. Although our ideal for poverty is the abandonment of Christ to the Father, each one's particular *symbolization* (lived-out expression) of this internalized attitude within the prescriptions of his congregation is unique and individual.

On the other hand, there also may be different expressions of poverty because of differing degrees of inner acceptance of its value. The liberty of heart which is necessary for the internalization[7] of the value of poverty finds its predispositions in each individual depending on, among other factors, the integration of psychic levels and the number of central subconscious conflicts and inconsistencies (i.e., major needs dissonant with vocational values).[8] Each one searches for freedom of heart, yet some are hampered by their own interior difficulties from responding fully. For this reason, exterior manifestations also differ since the value of poverty may be internalized to a differing degree in each person.

Fourthly and finally, poverty cannot be spoken of in isolated terms. We can, for purposes of discernment, focus on it—but we must relate it to community, celibacy, obedience, consecration to God, apostolic witness and service.[9] Why? Simply because the one and the same underlying symbolized relationship of love permeates each of the vows and acts of religion and finds complementarity in them. Only when one is open to both the desire and the imperfection in human love and friendship, can one choose to be celibate and offer the reality of this finiteness in the self-forgetfulness of the pure love of a religious.

The quality of our poverty, then, is also the quality of our obedience and chastity—it illuminates them both since it also bespeaks our abandonment and self-immolation in the area of the use of will and of sensual desire. As we will see presently, we cannot speak of abandonment or poverty of goods alone, as though the physical level functioned independently of other levels in our life. Abandonment also touches our psycho-social and spiritual-rational levels: we surrender goods, people and ourselves to Him; anything less than all this is only a partial gift.

Thus, as we mature, integrating hierarchically the three psychic levels within us (possible only if there are no serious vocational inconsistencies in us[10]), we can move more or less freely towards discovering the poverty of the human spirit in the face of the total claims of our transcendent God. The successful integration of all the levels predisposes us to a reaching out of self to God who freely chooses to take us up, to bend low and redeem us with His delicate, strong love. If, then, the internalization of the existential living of the vow of poverty for Christ depends on and flows from the psychic integration of the levels of a person, it is opportune here to go deeper into an understanding of these levels and their functions in us.

C. Predispositions to the Counsel of Poverty: The Levels of Psychic Life

All human beings respond to God through the psychological laws God has implanted in us.[11] I have noted on another occasion that the self is the meeting point of theology and psychology.[12] The "self" can be partitioned for purposes of understanding and insight. What are these distinct, yet unified levels of a person? How do they dispose us to poverty?

1. The Psycho-Physiological Level

We live on three levels, and each level has an implicit relationship to the experience of poverty in our lives. On the *first level*, we are physiological beings who need to sleep, eat and be healthy. Implicit in this biological-psychic structure of our life is the intuitive orientation for the right choice and use of the material goods which make survival and development possible. So already at this level, a kind of poverty is implied. In order to grow physiologically, in order to live, we are in need of such *things* as food, a place to sleep, clothes to protect us, money to purchase these goods, and all the rest. All these things need to be oriented and regulated, and used temperately, respectfully and wisely if we are to be healthy, vibrant beings, if we are to survive. Thus, our need for *things* is implicit in our physiological existence. We cannot pretend that we do not need things. "The existential need of the individual for material things is not merely a *de facto* one, but an essential aspect of our being as a spiritual person that is simultaneously spatio-temporal."[13] We need things ordered and integrated for existence and stability, so that maturation can occur effectively.

2. The Psycho-Social Level

The *second level* of our being is what we have called the psycho-social level: we are beings who need to have relationships with others, to be cared for by others, to be near others. Here we are faced with a new and qualitatively different dimension of poverty. We learn to value people (friends) above things, "being with" above "having." We learn to subordinate our desire for *things* on level one to our need for *people* on this second level. We need people because we are finite beings, limited in what we can do for ourselves and for others, and we learn to use material goods not merely for our own survival but also in respectful interaction with others. We are social beings and this implies a poverty.

3. The Spiritual-Rational Level

On the *third level*, we are spiritual-rational beings with needs to think, to judge, to evaluate, to go beyond the senses into abstraction, forming immaterial concepts about material things. Although each level presents needs which imply levels of even "natural" poverty, it is only through the third, the spiritual-rational level, that we begin to find within ourselves a capacity to discern a new, deeper, supernatural meaning of poverty. We are given the capacity to remove ourselves from the center of our own existence and affirm others, to reach out to God reaching out to us. That is, we can *choose* poverty, living it not only out of necessity for survival and growth (as on levels one and two), but out of desire for an ideal, i.e., as a value which touches the relationship with God. Through this level of our being, we see God's invitation to go beyond the materiality of things and the transitoriness of people, to commit ourselves to a relationship which transcends the functional, needy "me," and allows a "wise enjoyment and use of things not only in their immediacy (for themselves) but in their capacity to reveal the hidden, transcendent meaning of life and culture."[14] Through recollection, encounter, prayer, religious/ sacramental experiences, and a cognitive realization of our finiteness, we come to know God. We come to select that which can foster our own unique call and burning out of self (our gifts, our talents, our time) for this God, and we can detach ourselves from all that can obscure and destroy that fidelity, even if it be the needs of levels one and two. It is at this third level that we can take hold of our life and make the most of it for Him within the limits of our realistic possibilities.

This level enables us, or should enable us, to define *ourselves* in the light of our relationship to God. The intrinsic poverty of our finiteness and state of receptivity becomes evident. Through this level we can act from a *rational* wanting when we choose a value, not merely from an emotional need, or the desire for people or things, or our own self-interest.

Thus, on all three levels, poverty is indispensable. It can be the worst kind of self-deception to pretend we do not need the world in which God has put us—this is the beginning of pride, not humble poverty. These levels of existence in us, however, need to be integrated and hierarchically organized into a gradated poverty: from things—to people—to self-transcendence in love for God. Within ourselves we need to re-evaluate our needs on each level and determine if this hierarchical organization and direction is present in our lives of professed poverty. Let us re-examine the attitudes and practices of poverty possible on all these levels.

D. Uses and Abuses of the Counsel at the Various Levels

1. The Psycho-Physiological Level

The human attitude proper to this level implies, as we

mentioned, that we deal with things as oriented toward a specific need and goal: survival and development. However, when things and possessions become ends in themselves, when we seek to possess for security's sake (be it food, things, rest, and so forth), or for the sake of merely *having* rather than *surviving* and *developing*, a distortion of poverty is evident: there is an inversion of means and ends. Overuse becomes abuse and may be detrimental to ordered existence. For example, if pizza or candy is eaten to excess, health may actually be impaired rather than maintained and fostered. Van Kaam states:

> if the instinct of wise and right selection is not regulated by goals of maintenance and survival, the drive to select, gather, collect and use would take over totally, therefore no time, energy, attention would be left for the manifold other biological functions necessary for health, survival and creation. Without sobriety, the animal would destroy itself.[15]

Just naturally speaking, an imbalance would destroy rather than create.

If we consider the person as integrated, however—if we see him functioning with *all levels* of his being at the same time as an ordered unity—then we know that he can open up to others as well as to himself and to God. Then, the dimension of natural poverty expands. Things and survival itself at level one are seen not only in relationship to themselves or to others or to self, but in relation to the outpouring of the mystery of love between God and the person (third level). In this light, the attitude of poverty can take the stance of a counsel, of a transcendent attitude.

The third level predisposes us to embrace the attitudes of the other two levels and offers the opportunity for sanctification, i.e., self-transcendence. Our treatment of material goods, then, takes on new goals and perspectives: we seek to use them wisely, not merely for self-growth and survival (first level); not merely for communication, interaction and co-development with others (second level); but also through the third level as means to find Christ's love and to give ourselves to Him both in the gift of things and of persons. In the past, there was a trend to believe that possessions were of themselves an obstacle to union with Christ. The corollary followed, that the way of contemplation, of union with God, was simply the giving up of everything. This may or may not be true. On the other hand, the use of things (necessary, reasonable ones) may *not* be an obstacle but an opening to Christ's love—if oriented in a proper way to the goal for which they are given to us and which they can serve. This involves a dispossession, a generous gift of all that is entrusted to us. However, the dispossession of goods (as well as the use of things in a prudent way) will not necessarily lead to union with God if it is not Christ Himself who moves us to do this.

Underlying motivations are crucial here. If we choose to give away our goods to gain esteem in the eyes of others and thus make superficial friends and assure relationships rather than establishing true intimacy, the counsel of poverty is lost. If we pride ourselves on being "poorer" and thus somehow better than others, then too the counsel of poverty becomes a form of self-enhancement rather than a simple abandonment in trust to a loving Father. This is *compliance*, where rewards and punishments are the primary motivating factors. There may also be a type of *non-internalizing identification* underlying this action: I see some religious living a genuine poverty—I admire them and others do, too; I want to be poor like they are so that I, too, may be admired, or so that I can be close to them. Here, there is a subtle, social prestige or relationship I desire and, in this case, poverty can be a means to obtaining it. Being religiously poor, however, should stem from *internalization*, a value-expressive function of the counsel of poverty; that is, we deal with goods so as to manifest to others the truth that all things belong to Christ and find their meaning in him.

Concretely—then—if we *are* living as integrated beings with this internalized attitude of poverty, even on level one, would we expect the exterior manifestation of this attitude to be, for example, jealously hoarding our possessions; a harsh coldness when one asks for the car for apostolic reasons; too free a use and possession of a community car by one person; stinginess, keeping donations; a fanatic push to obtain the dress or book or crucifix or vacation that Sister or Brother or Father So-and-so has had; grumbling because of minor inconveniences? Hardly! Yes, we are called to share and to use the treasures the Lord has provided but are we going to become trapped in one isolated aspect of them? Will we center on our own development and security at level one, leaving levels two and three (others and God) unintegrated?

Our treatment of things can be a healing or divisive factor in our own personality or in the community. It is divisive when we perceive possessions and goods merely for the sake of our own security and are overwhelmed by a frenzy of collecting, preserving, manipulating. "Indiscriminate consumption, too, is the mask of a mindless personality who lives merely for fragmented moments of satisfaction."[16] The integrity of the whole person is eliminated when material goods become one's central fascination. This limits the richness of reality that can be found in internal integration and self-transcendence. We can easily limit ourselves to a *partial*, warped expression of the totality of our being. Through material goods, however, we might encounter ourselves and recognize our limitations and need for things, provided that our stance toward things is not greedy and grasping and does not supercede our interaction with people and our relationship with God. The internalized counsel or gift of poverty, then, can be healing—it can allow us to rise above the compulsion of our needs on level one in order to emerge as a whole person.

Travesties of the spirit of poverty in the use of goods can occur when 1) we must compulsively procure things (e.g., shopping becomes our major pastime); 2) we become permanently tied to the goods we have; 3) we are fixated on merely one dimension of their meaning, e.g., for our comfort or our survival alone. Have we really ever developed a respect for things as bespeaking God's practical generosity in loving us, or are they merely instruments of self-gratification? If it turns out to be only the latter, there results excessive obsession, and inability to give things away or to choose and use them wisely, and this can have the effect of making a virtue of selfishness: "I *might* need this—it's against poverty to get rid of it. . . ."

There can be no greater distortion of poverty, however, than to reduce the counsel to simply having or not having things. The deeper questions to be asked are: *Why* do I have this? *How much* do I want? What will I *do* with it? A return to the Gospels is imperative if we are to keep an objective motivation and balance: Christ makes available the finest wine at the wedding feast; He multiplies loaves, fills nets with fish; Mary Magdalene pours fragrant, expensive oils on Christ's feet. Yet, on the other hand, Christ has no place to lay His head, lives from a common purse, travels with no luggage, has His garments divided and is buried in a borrowed grave. Although it may seem a paradox, perhaps what is clear is that Christ did not identify with the prejudiced view of things and people and situations of those critics around Him. He saw life in deeper, cosmic terms, not in terms of survival, storing up, gratification, development. He evaluated things, people, self— integrating all levels of His humanity to the service of the manifestation of the will and love of a generous Father.

2. The Psycho-Social Level

What attitudes, then, could emerge through this second level of our being, the psycho-social level, which orientates us toward others? If this level acts in complementarity with level one as intended by the Divine Mind, people will be valued above things; our being and existence with others will be more valuable than merely having things. Just as with level one, however, we can fail to be integrated, leading a fragmented existence by depreciating or denying the other two levels, especially level three.

At this second level, possessiveness in regard to persons can enter in; elements of abandonment to trust in God and of response to His love through other persons can be left out. My time, thought, preoccupation turn out to be not an overt concern with goods alone for my own security and survival or development (as previously described in level one), but rather a real wish to make So-and-so happy. This is not bad. But is that all there is? *Must* I make him or her happy? Must I make him happy with *gifts*? Must I make him happy ultimately so he will be *mine*, so that I will receive from him? Where does God fit in all of this? Then, too, what about the attitude we hear so often: "They are giving to this or that family or parish or group but not to our community," or "They are giving more to one of the sisters/brothers/fathers than to me!" Are not our insecurities showing, our own fears of rejection, of being left out or depleted? Possessiveness is transferred from the area of things to that of persons. What happens, in such circumstances, to the basic faith in the fact that God reveals His providence through many, not merely one person (who must be grabbed onto)? Instead, we begin to learn to send out boomerangs—giving to others in order to get in return. Poverty then becomes utilitarian, i.e., useful for our need-gratification of level two only, not value-expressive as we profess through level three.

Do we value others because we vibrantly experience the supreme worth of Christ in them and the supreme value of belonging with them in Him? Should jealousy or envy be so evident in our lives? Or do we perhaps value specific people only for gratification of our need to be cared for, loved, accepted? Are we seeking to alleviate the material needs of humanity so as to minister to peoples' deep spiritual needs? This level challenges us to dispossess others by leaving them free in our love of them; and this must spring from a strong conviction of how much we need Christ above all, how firmly Christ possesses us and how carefully He watches over His own. Our poverty, then, is a means by which we can regulate the underlying psychological needs of level two. One author summarizes this well:

> In order to transcend narrowness, an individual must examine his tendency to clutch others as if they were possessions. A parent who is too strict, a lover constantly agitated by jealousy, a person who has become so dependent on someone else that he feels no identity except through the other, must learn what it means to let go.[17]

Only in letting go for Christ can one discover the capacity he has within himself to enrich others and be truly enriched by them.

Poverty on this second level, in the light of the third, can mean experiencing at the gut level of our being the gnawing anxiety of being separated and alone, and, at the same time, of struggling to love freely and unreservedly and faithfully so that others, too, may exist and develop and love freely. It can mean experiencing the excruciating emptiness of rejection by family, being ignored or forgotten even temporarily by friends, criticized by enemies; on the other hand, it can mean choosing to offer to others the enriching love of one's friends, the generosity of one's family and encouragement from acquaintances, inspiration from others with whom I share. It can mean living alone, when circumstances so require it, in a *creative* aloneness; it can mean living intimately near, if situations allow it. And through it all, it always means being flexible—being totally available despite emotional desires, indiscriminately accepting loss and change, or persevering in and deepening relationships for Christ. Religious community becomes not merely a "social convenience" or gratification but, as Rahner puts it, a "means of serving *him*, continuing *his* life and witnessing to its power." It is a *means*—a coming together in vocation to better fulfill *this* mission of crucifixion and resurrection. "We are enriched by such a community," he says, "only to the extent we try to give (to that mission) more than to receive."[18]

3. *The Spiritual-Rational Level*

We spoke of the third psychic level within us as disposing us to rational wanting, the capacity in us for judging, valuing, abstracting, transcending, going beyond ourselves. Because of this innate gift, needs of other levels can be regulated and integrated. Because of this level, the God-man and supernatural elements can touch our lives and enter our hearts. The counsel of poverty thus can elevate the natural needs and set them correctly in their hierarchy of created order. We can forget *ourselves*. The attitude and abandonment of this level underlines not merely dispossession of others for our own good and theirs (level two), but opens us up to the possibility of dispossession of even *ourselves* for Him. That is, surrender to Providence finds its sequel in surrender of one's own life, including one's own time, qualities, name, status, and power, in loving service of Him and others. Let us look more carefully into these.

Dispossession of one's life. If we are totally possessed by and given to Christ, we cannot withhold ourselves in any manner from Him. Therefore, most basically, do I care to preserve my health and, if in ill-health, do I do what is required to regain it; and if I am beset with chronic ailments, do I offer to others and to God the limitations of my corporeal finiteness as a manifestation of faith in a richness which lies beyond all bodily functions? Am I really in constant touch with my conviction that even my next breath depends on God? Am I willing to be available to *change* my personality if I see it hindering God's work?

Speaking of life's insecurities, how often we find ourselves faltering and complaining pessimistically about the lack of vocations, being sent to an undesirable place, given undesirable work! This is an actual poverty which results in painful insecurity, indeed—and who wants to suffer the pain of insecurity? Only if we choose to make of it a creative religious experience of humble faith will it have meaning, will we be like Christ, dispossessing ourselves of our own lives as He did.

Dispossession of one's time. Is there a proper balance of my time between relaxation for regeneration and working in a spirit of co-creation with Him? Is my time used profitably, or wasted on cheap, shallow interests which are rationalized away as "others are doing it," "it's for the apostolate," "teachers, nurses, and so forth, should be exposed to these things"? Would a statement like "I have it coming to me after twenty-five years in Community; I earned it!" be compatible with a "no strings attached" surrender of my time to Him, or does it perhaps betray an underlying attitude of bartering rather than of abandonment? In a word, as one priest puts it: "Have I written *Jesus Christ* on the page of each day of the year that just passed?"[19]

Dispossession of one's qualities. Total surrender to Providence also finds its sequel in the surrender of one's own qualities in loving service of Him and others. If we find ourselves graced with a sensitive heart, a flair for entertaining and regaling on occasion, an ear for listening, a mind for analyzing, a capacity for organizing, it is imperative that we offer these, making the most of ourselves for Him within the limit of our potentialities. We can waste our lives if we refuse to offer ourselves. A growing feeling of boredom, apathy, or cynicism, meaninglessness and despair soon replace the vibrant hope of sharing somehow with God in creating, in renewing hope and enthusiasm through the gifts of personal, God-given qualities. Furthermore, whether or not this offering, this willing surrender of one's talents to the service of the Church is accepted, understood, or rejected, the gift is nevertheless given attitudinally. Humility and faith can best grow if there is a ground of unconditional, selfless motivation in the gift of one's qualities.

Dispossession of one's name, status, power. Through level three, we are able, as we said, to arrive at a poverty which is able to detach itself from surface appearances and commune with the transcendent meaning of self, persons and things.[20] This concern with inner meaning distances one from the mere immediate symbol, the immediate cause, the material and practical meaning of things and social relationships. In this centering on God, one's name, status, and power, i.e., one's desire to be "in" with the establishment, becomes less significant. Christ indicates the way: "As for human approval, this means nothing to me" (Jn 5:41). Constant awareness of our own weakness, our inner poverty will bring us to the feet of Christ and assist us to distance ourselves from preoccupation with mere profit, gain, and high social esteem, [21] all of which condition a false, unstable self-esteem. If we can see and treat each other in terms of who we are in ourselves, regardless of name or power, accepting our own and others' gifts and limitations in humble gratitude and satisfaction, we will have no need for fanatic drives to establish, manipulate for and maintain a good name, some status or power. Those alone need to parade their name or status or power who lack inner depth and feel frantically insecure.

The same is true for those who need to criticize and depreciate others constantly. Perhaps this indicates dissatisfaction with one's own efforts, and a narcissistic anger with God who is loving the other in a different way—in a way, we feel, "better" than the way He is loving us. This questions God's justice as well as His personal love for us; this puts our "lower" levels of existence first, that is, ourselves and our needs. This is not being "poor" as Christ was poor.

Especially these days, there is an unconscious motive frequently seen in some to build their lives on desires for measurable achievement—professional capacity rather than *religious living*. For many, efficiency is more important than effectiveness. However, as religious, we are not called to serve the functional needs of society only. There are others able to do that. We *do* need to radically live our human and spiritual values wherein all true riches lie. The English psychiatrist Dominian sees it clearly: "The fuller a person becomes in his own experience of himself [in this present work we have called it self- or level-integration and order], the less he needs or envies material goods or social advantages which enhance his identity."[22] Merton, too, emphasized that ". . . man must become detached from all the illusions that he has fabricated about his selfish and limited self. This kind of renunciation underscores the necessity of self-emptying of one's external and false self so as to become aware of man's inner self as well as God."[23] He describes this beautifully:

> The path to transcendent realization is a path of ascetic self-emptying and "self-naughting" and not at all a path of self-affirmation, of self-fulfillment or of "perfect attainment . . ." Hence, it becomes overwhelmingly important for us to become detached from our everyday conception of ourselves as potential subjects for special and unique experiences, or as candidates for realization, attainment and fulfillment.[24]

Along these lines, let us also consider possession of the past, or of the present, or of the future. If we are unconcerned with our own need for self-gratification, we will not focus our lives only on the past—what we did not receive, nor on the present—what we are not receiving, nor on the future—what we will receive. A real poverty implies a humble need to forgive others for being humanly limited *as we are*, to accept all that happens to us as momentarily God's manifest hand of love in our daily living. Forgiveness springs from a solid integration of all levels of our being. If we were poor in our interior attitude and thus humble in forgiving, would we find hostile, grandiose silences and refusals to talk to others in community so frequently? We must look forward to creating for the future rather than hoarding in the present and bemoaning the past: "forgiveness is the way we bless the future and make provision for it."[25]

Thus poverty is an invaluable means to proper discernment of values in our religious calling. With a humble attitude of awe in the face of God's tremendous love for us and the total response of all levels of our being to that love we distance ourselves from things, others, ourselves, and integrate and order the levels of our being for Him, and in Him. This prevents fragmentation of our being. Poverty focuses our attention on God above all else. It prevents preoccupation with level one or level two rather than integration and organization of all levels through level three in the light of grace. This healing results in preventing us from becoming enslaved to our personal needs, desires, and interests. Seen in this way, poverty is liberating, freeing, enriching. Asserting his material claims, the *rich* person's trend is to become full of himself and dazed by power, prestige, esteem, and adulation from others. Impatience, then, becomes characteristic of the rich person; the pain and discomfort of aloneness, insecurity in religious life are seen only in terms of absence and deprivation, not in terms of the possibility for joyous co-creation and creativity through a hierarchical ordering and harmonious blending of all levels of our being in response to Christ's presence.

E. Criteria for Evaluating One's Personal Spirit of Religious Poverty

Having now discussed some concepts and their concrete applications, we can condense our considerations into certain general criteria by which we can evaluate our personal spirit of religious poverty.

1. Congruity:

a) Is our poverty congruous with the example of Christ? If we, in simple profound terms, wish to be poor, there is no clearer, general criteria to be used than those found in the Gospels and the example of Christ as mentioned at the outset.

b) Furthermore, this following of Christ is more specifically elaborated in our Constitutions or Ecclesial Exhortations. Do we respond to these prescriptions with love, fear, or a side-stepping of them?

c) Another whole area to be considered is congruency of our poverty in the social situation in which we find ourselves. Does our possession or dispossession of material goods indicate an identification with the poor? Do we have a more vital sensitivity to the frustrations and insecurities of the humanly destitute, whatever be their social or economic status?

2. Which level of our being?

From a psychological perspective, we need to consider which level of being expressed through poverty is major in our lives. A natural concern with dispossession of goods and people, that is, levels one and/or two, to the exclusion of three; level one alone—goods; level two alone—people; or are all levels subordinated to and integrated in level three which allows and assists us to respond to Christ's call to transcendence, to loving, humble, total abandonment? Does our attitude of poverty stem from a personal need in us only, or an objective value?

3. Which process of our psyche?

Is our poverty prompted, motivated by compliance, that is, a wish to please others or avoid criticism and punishment, a wish to be accepted? Or perhaps, is it motivated by non-internalizing identification, that is, a wish to be like another for the gain in self-esteem or social benefits it brings? Is it truly internalization? Do we choose poverty because we are driven to it by our conflicting needs or because of the social rewards we get from it, rather than because it is valuable in itself as a means of total response to God's loving call to union with Him, amidst all the insecurities and limitations of our created-ness?

4. Which functions?

Poverty can serve different functions. Is it:

a) *utilitarian*, that is, for me? I give gifts to get them in return, or give up things to be thought well of and admired. I hand in my donations to avoid being questioned about it.

b) Perhaps it is *ego-defensive*. I give gifts and live poorly, for example, to build my self-esteem. I like to feel better than the religious next to me. Perhaps I deprive myself of something out of guilt for my 'cheating' in other areas of religious living or other aspects of poverty (e.g., holding on possessively to a dependent relationship).

c) Perhaps it is *knowledge-oriented*. I want to become poor as the poor, to understand their insecurity and frustration.

d) Or is it truly *value-expressive*, indicative of an outpouring from an intense love-relationship with the Beloved, a spontaneous attempt to preserve, nourish and expand that loving surrender to Christ?

5. Which procedure of evaluation do I use?

a) *Emotional wanting*, that is, I give and renounce and use what I want when I *feel* like doing it, when I am fearful, when I am guilty, when I am elated, inspired or loved; when things are going well.

b) *Rational wanting*: I give and renounce and use everything always to the measure and in the manner God's will indicates out of a growing *conviction* rather than a temporary sentiment.

6. Which fruits are evident?

Am I *humble* enough to admit sincerely my limitations or do I blame them on others? A true spirit of poverty will manifest itself in greater warmth, openness, detachment, creativity; whereas greed breeds boredom, cynicism, isolation, hardness of heart, self-centeredness.

Conclusion

Thus poverty is an invaluable means to proper discernment of values in our religious calling: with a humble attitude of awe in the face of God's tremendous love for us and the total response of all levels of our being to that love, we distance ourselves enough from things, others, ourselves, and integrate and order the levels of our being. This prevents fragmentation of our being (i.e., preoccupation with goods or persons or self rather than with God) and it heals; it prevents us from becoming enslaved by our personal needs, desires and interests. Seen in this way, poverty is liberating, directing, freeing, enriching.[26]

So we arrive at the end of our considerations. More can be said; but what is to be done? We can be content to beat our breasts in passive shame for our limitedness in true poverty. We can put this book down with a gentle musing: "interesting . . . Amen." Father Byron, in an article on discernment, suggests that if ours is the attitude of passivity, it is the first indication that we are not really poor, for discernment and evaluation demand some poverty already as a prerequisite—an openness, a humility to search for our limitations and right them.[27]

Each one of us, then, needs to personally work with persevering determination to make real the apostolic exhortation of Pope Paul:

> In a civilization and a world marked by a prodigious movement of almost indefinite material growth, what witness would be offered by a religious who let himself be carried away by an uncurbed seeking for his own ease, and who considered it normal to allow himself without discernment or restraint everything that is offered to him? At a time when there is an increased danger for many of being enticed by the alluring security of possessions, knowledge, and power, the call of God places you at the pinnacle of the Christian conscience. You are to remind men that their true and complete progress consists in responding to their calling "to share as sons in the light of the living God, the father of all men."[28]

Merton's writing on the transformation of our consciousness somehow delicately points to the same instrumental role of poverty in our lives: "But indeed we exist solely for this, to be the place he has chosen for his presence, his manifestation in the world; his epiphany. . . . Love is the epiphany of God in our poverty."[29] It is emptiness like the hollow in the reed, the narrow, riftless emptiness which can have only one destiny: to receive the piper's breath and to sing with our Lady her Magnificat.[30] True freedom, the freedom of poverty, means that, free from all ties within our "self," we take account of the true hierarchy of levels, of values visualized in a supernatural light (the "one thing necessary"), and adjust all our attachments to them, so that in having Him we have nothing else but all things in Him and epiphany besides!

Footnotes

1. Abbott, pp. 475 ff. "Decree On The Appropriate Renewal of Religious Life."
2. Thomas Clarke, "Witness and Involvement." *The Way Supplement*, 1970, 9, p. 49.
3. Ladislas Orsy, "Poverty: The Modern Problem." *The Way Supplement*, 1970, 9, p. 11.
4. Clarke, op. cit.
5. Thomas Clarke, "Discerning the Ignatian Way in Poverty Today." *The Way Supplement*, 1973, 19, p. 95.
6. W. Yeomans, "Come Follow Me." *The Way Supplement*, 1970, 9, p. 58.
7. Internalization is the process of adopting a way of behavior or thinking because it is congruent with one's value system and/or with objective Gospel values rather than with any rewards it might bring. From Rulla, Ridick and Imoda, p. 397.
8. For further explanation of the theory of central subconscious conflicts and inconsistencies see L.M. Rulla, *Depth Psychology and Vocation: A Psycho-social Perspective*, (Rome: Gregorian University Press, 1971). See also Rulla, Ridick and Imoda.
9. Clarke, "Discerning the Ignatian Way . . ."
10. Rulla, *Depth, Psychology and Vocation* . . . and Rulla, Ridick and Imoda.
11. Ibid.
12. Sr. Joyce Ridick, "Value Orientation and Discernment." *Review for Religious*, 1976, 35, pp. 914-927.
13. J.J. Sikora, "Poverty Today." *Review for Religious*, 1967, 26, p. 4.
14. Adrian Van Kaam, *The Vowed Life*, (Denville, N.J.: Dimension Books, 1968), p. 215.
15. Ibid., p. 22.
16. Ibid., p. 130.

17. E.M. Stern and B.G. Marino. *Psychotheology*, (New York: Newman Press, 1970), p. 78.
18. Karl Rahner, *The Religious Life Today*, (London: Burns & Oates, 1977).
19. Rev. Stanley Gaucias, Unpublished manuscript. (Chicago, Illinois, 1975).
20. Van Kaam, p. 304.
21. M. Ivens, "Religious Poverty in Contemporary Writing." *The Way Supplement*, 1970, 9, p. 81.
22. J. Dominian, "Formation of a Celibate." Unpublished Conference. (London, England: 1975), p. 15.
23. J. Higgins, *Thomas Merton on Prayer*, (Garden City, New York: Doubleday, 1975).
24. Thomas Merton, *Zen and the Birds of Appetite*, (New York: New Directions, 1968), pp. 76-77.
25. Stern and Morino, p. 98.
26. W.J. Byron, "Discernment and Poverty," *The Way Supplement*, 1974, 23, p. 39.
27. Ibid.
28. Apostolic Exhortation: *On the Renewal of Religious Life According to the Teaching of the Second Vatican Council*, (Boston: St. Paul Editions, 1971), p. 16.
29. Higgins, pp. 69-70.
30. Caryll Houselander, *The Reed of God*, (New York: Arena Lettres, 1978), p. 1.

Bibliography

Abbott, W.M. (S.J.) Ed. *The Documents of Vatican II*. Decree on the Appropriate Renewal of Religious Life. New York: Guild Press, 1966, pp. 475ff.

Albrecht, Barbara. Evangelical Poverty. *Review for Religious*. 1977, 36, 6, pp. 918-923.

Apostolic Exhortation: *On the Renewal of Religious Life According to the Teaching of the Second Vatican Council*. Boston: St. Paul Editions, 1971, p. 16.

Arrupe, Pedro (S.J.). Simplicity of Life. *Sursum Corda*. Oct., 1974, pp. 212-224.

Byron, W.J. Discernment and Poverty. *The Way Supplement*. 1974, 23, p. 39.

Clarke, Thomas (S.J.). Discerning the Ignatian Way in Poverty Today. *The Way Supplement*. 1973, 19, pp. 88-95.

_____. Witness and Involvement. *The Way Supplement*. 1973, 19, p. 95.

_____. Witness and Involvement. In *New Pentecost or New Passion. The Direction of Religious Life Today*. New York: Paulist Press, 1973, pp. 82-94.

D'Arc, Sr. Jeanne (O.P.). La Povertà. In Tillard, J. (O.P.), and Congar, Y. (O.P.), *Il Rinnovamento Della Vita Religiosa*. Firenze: Valecchi, 1968, pp. 356-390.

Emery, Andrée. On Religious Poverty. *Communio: International Catholic Review*. Spring 1982, pp. 16-21.

Gaucias, Rev. Stanley. Unpublished manuscript. Chicago, Illinois: 1975.

Genovesi, V. Christian Poverty: Sign of Faith and Redemptive Force. *The Way Supplement*. 1977, 32, pp. 78-82.

Higgins, J. *Thomas Merton on Prayer*. Garden City, New York: Doubleday, 1975.

Ivens, M. (S.J.). Religious Poverty in Contemporary Writing. *The Way Supplement*. 1970, 9, p. 81.

Knight, David M. (S.J.). *Cloud by day, fire by night: the meaning and choice of religious poverty*. Vol. II. A publication of the Canadian Religious Conference, 324 Laurier Avenue East, Ottawa, Canada K1N 6P6. *"Vita Evangelica."* Series, no. 11, 1979.

Merton, Thomas (O.C.S.O.). *Zen and the Birds of Appetite*. New York: New Directions, 1968, pp. 76-77.

Metz, Johannes B. *Poverty of Spirit*. New York: Paulist Press, 1968.

O'Connor, J. (O.P.). Poverty and Community. *Supplement to Doctrine and Life*. 1973, II, 3, pp. 40-52.

Orsy, Ladislas (S.J.). Poverty: The Modern Problem. *The Way Supplement*. 1970, 9, p. 49.

Rahner, K. (S.J.). *The Religious Life Today*. New York: Crossroad Publ. Co., 1976.

Ridick, Sr. Joyce (S.S.C.). Value Orientation and Discernment. *Review for Religious*. 1976, 35, pp. 914-927.

Rulla, L.M. (S.J.). *Depth Psychology and Vocation: a psycho-social perspective*. Rome: Gregorian University Press, 1971.

Rulla, L.M. (S.J.), Ridick, Sr. Joyce, (S.S.C), Imoda, F. (S.J.). *Entering and Leaving Vocation: Intrapsychic Dynamics*. Rome: Gregorian University Press, and Chicago: Loyola University Press, 1980.

Sikora, J.J. (S.J.). Poverty Today. *Review for Religious*. 1967, 26, p. 4.

Stern, E.M. and Marino, B.G. *Psychotheology*. New York: Newman Press, 1970.

Thirty Second General Congregation (Jesuit). Poverty. *The Way Supplement*. 1977, 29-30, pp. 73 ff.

Van Breeman, P.G. *Called by Name*. Denville, New Jersey: Dimension Books, 1976, pp. 229-235.

Van Kaam, A. (C.S.Sp.). *The Vowed Life*. Denville, New Jersey: Dimension Books, 1968.

Yeomans, W. Come Follow Me. *The Way Supplement*. 1970, 9, p. 58.

CHAPTER II

CHASTITY

"This is my Body, broken for you . . ."

I. INTRODUCTION

Thomas Merton wrote, "He who attempts to act and do for others, or for the world, without deepening his own self-understanding, freedom, integrity, and capacity to love, will not have anything to give others. He will communicate to them nothing but the contagion of his own obsessions, his aggressivity, his ego-centered ambition, his delusions about ends and means."[1] In the light of this quote, it would seem that each reader would desire self-renewal in the gift of chastity. It has been years, perhaps, since we studied this vow, one of the three essential treasures of our life. Perhaps we have forgotten what we learned, or new questions have arisen out of our experiences. It is important to re-evaluate ourselves, to ask not only about celibacy itself, but how things are going with *my* celibacy. Does it witness to Christ or to my own egoism? It is important to see how we are living the inevitable choice of chastity which came with our call to religious life and what attitude we have taken toward it. What *real* value does it have in our lives? We need to polish up the "diamond" and let it sparkle. It is not a cumbersome burden or a forgotten relic but a precious jewel. In these days of sexual liberty, pornography, indulgence, where do we place our vow of total surrender, of modest continency, of renunciation? Is it inhuman? Was our training too "rigid" in this sphere? Have "the rules" changed?

First we will define the natural elements which constitute us as human beings. Then we will explore how the supernatural vow of chastity is founded on the natural elements and sustained in them. This will involve a discussion, of course, of *love* as a unifying, sacralizing factor in the natural and divine. We will consider different types of love which are possible: the ideal we strive for as well as the other options possible. By this time, a definition of chastity with clear distinctions should emerge. This is the diamond! What use is it? What does it *mean* today, in the world which offers so many other "treasures" for the asking? We will consider, therefore, the witness value of this vow, and from there move into the problems which can, or perhaps *have* arisen to cloud the crystal clarity of the jewel and trouble us. We will conclude by analyzing a few means which we can use to re-vitalize our vow of chastity and its effects.

II. LOVE:

A. Defining Human Elements in Love

Who are we, as religious, as persons? How "wonderfully made" we are, as the Psalmist proclaims. Let's look at God's loving wisdom in creating us and examine the different levels of our living, thinking, acting, and how they relate to our sexual being.

To begin with, we are beings who live on three natural levels. If we look at any of our ordinary acts, we can find any or all of these three elements in them: the psycho-physiological level, the psycho-social level, and the spiritual-rational level.

1. The Psycho-physiological Level

We are organic, psycho-physiological beings. We have chemical rhythms and physiological reactions. We need to eat, to sleep. We react with our senses and feelings. We feel drawn to touch, to be touched, to be filled, and to be delighted sensually. For example, we not only need food and feel hungry but we like the taste of food. Also, at certain times of the month or day, in certain seasons of the year and stages of life, sexual impulses or "instincts" are stronger. Not only do we have bodily needs, but also we are present to ourselves, and to others, in a bodily sense. As Van Kaam puts it: "My body invests my world with meaning even before I think about this meaning. It imposes a meaning on things which is not the imposition of meaning on the world by my consciousness."[2] For example, at age twenty the body acts and reacts to the world with intensity, involvement, movement, seeing the world as something to be conquered. At the age of eighty the body is more detached, moves slowly, with more caution and uncertainty, seeing the world as something to be offered. This means I am not necessarily free on this level of my body, capable of determining its precise meaning; rather, it just "happens." In regards to chastity, genital desire or erection can come spontaneously, in a dream, before a menstrual period, or while watching a movie or reading a book. We "feel" the experience of it as something good, warm, tender, and we desire it without specifically thinking about it. It is an emotional, physiological pull. Our bodies have physiological needs which establish a preconscious dialogue between ourselves and the world. The body can activate and facilitate interaction between ourselves and others, preparing itself by posture, by warmth, by attention, by softness or hardness for the emotionally, physiologically, sexually appealing or sexually repelling object.

At the physiological level, before any reflection, we are spontaneously attracted towards what is perceived as "good." Sometimes this "good" may be an undefined, global "good" or desire; at other times it may be specific, for example, desire for one particular person or a particular kind of experience. Interestingly, however, these physiological states of desire or arousal are of limited duration. For example, when the menstrual period arrives, the acuteness of desire subsides; the movie scene is over, and the warmth recedes, just as unintentionally as it came; the attractive person passes, and we calm down. Interestingly also, fatigue or frustration can dull the senses or limit their effectiveness in transmitting signals and determining meaning; all orgasms naturally come to a moment of exhaustion and conclusion. Thus, our bodies are drawn to and repelled from persons, situations, objects which can be satisfying or fulfilling in a bodily way. Man wants physically to fill, woman to be filled; both want to excite and be excited.

In and through the body, the other, the world is given to me, becomes in some sense mine, is engulfed in my need, my desire. Although such spontaneous meaning does exist at this level, this meaning of bodily satiation or excitement is not strictly characteristic of human beings. Animals have similar needs which are non-reflective, spontaneous, automatic. They are emotionally drawn towards or away from objects or situations which are physically harmful or desirable. Our bodies too are *made* to react, to sense, to feel, to search, to be satisfied. The word "carnal" is often applied to this kind of attraction or "love" as desire of the senses.[3] In this way somatic and physiological changes and processes, arising simply as response to stimuli, and so without our control or processing as a person, condition the value of the body and of sex. We come to accept and value our bodies as a necessary means of dialogue, of satisfaction, of pleasure. We can, as human beings, love others' bodies, touch them for the same reason. Therefore sensual excitability is innate and natural; it is neither morally good nor morally evil,[4] it just *is*. Every direct contact has an immediate sense reaction, that is, the sense impression is accompanied by emotion, by desire for fulfillment, for satisfaction. Sensuality is not only a simple reaction of the senses to the object, it consists in the experience of definite *values*, perceptible by the senses, even if these values are simply the value of the body of the other person, or the value of one's own body.[5] We have, then, a natural desire of the senses and a perception or image of our own body and of the bodies of others as objects of spontaneous pleasure.

Whether a person is nearby or absent, his body or hers can be a value for us as a possible object of pleasure. Our body can be the same for ourselves, an object of pleasurable sensations. This is a biochemical sense experience with an emotional cause and effect. This is a basic level of every human and every animal. From this it is evident that human beings can never fully understand their sexuality or the world unless they profoundly appreciate their own body first,[6] unless they perceive meaning in it and put meaning into it. However, sex is also *different* in the human being. Whereas other physiological needs such as eating and sleeping possess no special significance for the human person since they are self-contained, that is, they are not means for entering into a relationship, the same is not true of sex.[7] Why? For human beings sex is not just physiological, not self-contained on this one level, not merely to satisfy one's own physiological need; other levels of the person are also involved. Still, on this first level, we seek primarily to touch, to hold, to be touched; to give so as to be stimulated, excited, pleased. Sexual attraction may be love; here "love" is merely sympathy, the fruit of a need, of affective physiological experience.[8]

2. The Psycho-social Level

The second level is the psycho-social level. We are beings who have need for social contact, for acceptance, for recognition, for interaction and communication; we need love and care and attention. We are limited in what we can do and be for ourselves; we are created to grow through interaction with others, through closeness with others. We learn through the complementarity of each other: what I cannot do or have or be for myself, the other may be or have or do for me, and teach me. On this level the focus of attention shifts from my own or the other's *bodily* presence and gratification and communication to a higher form of "being with" some other more totally. My vision is expanded beyond *self*-preservation and *self*-satisfaction to self-affirmation through cooperation with others.

Whereas on level one, existence and relation were often based on "sympathy," i.e. subjective meaning, attractiveness, spontaneous physical evaluation for my own good; on this second level, camaraderie or relationship may be founded on common grounds such as work, common goals, interests. Thus a more objective element is brought into our being-in-the-world: there is a goal beyond my own physical well-being; there is an element of union of wills for a common endeavor. There is another object outside myself. Love, on this level, involves some *will*, not merely attraction; it is the fruit of voluntary acts and choices, not merely of physical experience or stimulation.[9] An "object" becomes "the" object, defined, formed, differentiated as a specific "other," with characteristics all his or her own. This level allows the formation of real "friendship," where recognition of the value of the other as object outside of me is possible. A real benevolence, or wishing well, to one's own more encompassing real self, as well as to the *other* apart from oneself, is the core potential at this level.

While sympathy or attraction on level one is subjective and physical, friendship on the second level is a bit more objective, not restricted only to instinct or impulse. This level brings to love or friendship or sexual relation an element of responsibility. Wojtyla says "man is not responsible for what *happens* in him in the sphere of sex [as on level one, in the body] since he is obviously not himself the cause of it, but he *is* entirely responsible for what he *does* in this field."[10] We might add, then, as an example on level two, that there is *responsibility* in social relationships. Relationships can include sexual beings but need not be "sexy," i.e., relationships need not be driven by or focalized primarily on the sexual characteristics or sexual instincts as in level one. We can love as a sexual man or woman, not as a sexed "object," and focus on the more advanced personal well-being of both parties in the relationship. Social goals and persons become more important elements in our presence to the world than mere bodily pleasure or satisfaction. Physical attraction may be subsumed into broader goals and visions, which may imply refocalizing one's physical tendencies.

Thus, level two confers on the individual the possibility of completing oneself reciprocally, but in a social reciprocity that is psychic rather than physical. Here we come to know the limitedness, the contingency of our own being, our insufficiency as *persons*. We cannot do or be everything alone. We need each other. Man's strength needs woman's delicateness, and strength and delicateness here mean more than physical strength or delicateness. This complementarity is not merely a man-woman thing;

the talents of one woman must be rounded out by the gifts of another woman. No man (or woman) is an island. Therefore love and sexuality here move from physical instinctual gratification to social coexistence and well-being.

The spontaneous "exteriority" of stimulus-response or emotion and sensuality characteristic of the first level shifts on the second level to a more complete "interiority," an affectivity that is not merely body-oriented. This stimulus begins to be processed through more of our person. While the initial contact with the world may be physical and sensual, a deeper form of being present to the world comes with the capacity to be *with* others, to be *near* them not simply for the satisfaction of one's own physical needs. Objective elements, such as the goals of apostolic work, may serve to limit or "correct" subjective, intuitive, sensual evaluations and idealizations made at the first level;[11] for example, though a person may be physically appealing, they may lack the necessary qualities for collaborating in teaching mathematics or doctrine or in nursing work. Thus, body-attraction may give way to goal-orientation or personal well-being. One seeks not merely to give and get physically, but to give and get what each person *has* and does, including ideas, visions of the world, goals, methods, sentiments, etc. Looks, words, gestures, are now more person-oriented; affectivity enters in, not mere sensuality. Affectivity is the facility (as distinct from the mere excitability of the first level) to react to the sexual values of the person in *all* his or her complexity, to react to femininity or masculinity.[12] It is a willed response which can bring people close to each other even when absent from each other. One recalls the person in all his/her characteristics, not merely the physical. Horizons are expanded.

We have seen, so far, that we need to integrate sympathy or attractedness (level one) to a more objective benevolence of choice, of self-determination in friendship (level two), allowing *reason* to enter in more where *emotion* wishes to reign, letting *people* be more important than physical gratification or perfection; to grow in interiority, in inner-directedness, rather than to respond only in an exterior fashion for immediate self-gratification or fulfillment.

From where does this deepened interiority come? From our third level of existing: the spiritual-rational level.

3. The Spiritual-rational Level

On the third level, the spiritual-rational level, we find our innate created need to think, to judge, to evaluate, to go beyond the material, present, immediate senses, to form concepts which are immaterial and more lasting. We reflect on ends and means and *choose*. While level one and level two in our existence automatically imply some "sexual" relationships, one as physical, the other as social, the third level opens up to us another possibility and horizon. Because we can reason and form concepts we can come to some desire for transcendence, for going beyond our own needs, even the sexual ones on one or the other level and at times even the social ones. This allows genuine altruistic love which is distinctively human because it is based on a truth outside of one's own needs, a value beyond oneself. This level takes us into the invisible world of the spiritual, of love, of truth, of goodness for its own sake. Thus, we are freed from biological determinism or social utilitarianism.

We can evaluate the "sexual" attraction as: 1) a good for me physically, here and now (level one); 2) a good for a common mission or social interaction (level two); or 3) a good for long-range values which may not be socially or physically satisfying. Thus, the third level raises love to a qualitatively different stance: it may move from friendship or love of benevolence (giving one's goods or plans or what one *has*) to a more perfect love of devotion, i.e. giving all one *has*, all one *is*, directly, absolutely, and without conditions.[13] In this way, for example, I may hold someone's hand, yet not give her my plan of life (level one); I may give her my plan of life and hold her hand (level two) yet not be totally available to her; or, finally, I may be totally available spiritually, physically, socially, offering her my total spirit or soul, my entire being. Maritain calls this last form of love "amore folle" or "mad love." The spirit can, through this third level, raise itself outside the flesh or passion or mutuality to a more authentic, extreme and radical kind of love.[14] The person can make him- or herself a total, unique gift, without reserve. Thus the *quality* of love changes. I can love not for physical or social completion, but rather can "alienate" my soul, by choice, from myself, and lay it down for another. This level allows me to go beyond a partial interaction with the other in his/her body or merely as a person capable of social interaction, and to see others apart from myself, as good in themselves, not for what benefit I can get from them. Thus, this level underlines even more the *will* factor in the sensual, affective interaction. It is a maturing of love.

Wojtyla says: "*Love is only psychologically complete when it possesses a moral value*, when it is a virtue"[15] focusing on the person not as an object of pleasure (physical or social) but as objectively good in himself. This involves a gift of self which is spiritual or moral, not merely a physical gift of self or a psychological gift of self for some mutual gain. It is a gift of one's soul. To give oneself entirely is more than to "wish one well." We can transcend ourselves. Victor Frankl, speaking of real love, says: "Love is really one aspect of a more encompassing human phenomenon which I have come to call self-transcendence . . . man is, by virtue of the self-transcendent quality of the human reality, basically concerned with reaching out beyond himself, be it toward a meaning to fulfill, or toward another human being lovingly to encounter."[16] This is transcendence, but it is still merely a human transcendence: I leave myself in love for another human person. Yet another potential is involved in this level and this is a self-transcendence oriented not only toward human objects, but a self-transcendence reaching out toward the Divine, God.

This level allows us to realize that we do not derive our existence from ourselves: our first cause is *outside* ourselves and it is this relationship which is primary. Thus this third level of self-transcendence enables us to understand and perceive that it is the love of the Creator (not our own love or that of others) that has decided our existence and sustains it. The order of existence, then, is seen as a divine order, although existence as such is not supernatural. Existence is, in fact, both natural and supernatural.[17] Love, too, can be both natural, directed toward creatures, and supernatural, directed toward the Creator. We can reflect, choose goals and means beyond our physical or social needs; we can love not merely with the body for pleasure, nor merely with our "personality" for social pleasure or material or psychic gain; we can also love with our embodied souls, even when self-gain as pleasure or satisfaction is not forthcoming.

Due to a deepened interiority at this level, in view of a greater good, I can, at times, *not will* what I desire or what others desire of me at another level. In this way freedom is allowed, real freedom, and the maturity of the person. As one author puts it: "A mature person can use affective energy with liberty and responsibility, towards real, altruistic ideals, ideals which are holocausts. Feelings and images [on the other two levels] when holocaustic, are synthesized into the spiritual: thus living out the depth of transcendence of the spiritual being."[18] We are freed to order desires, objects, persons and ideals: to pass from part-human objects or relationships, used for our own satisfaction, to human objects or relationships which meet our desire for self-fulfillment, and to human-divine objects or relationships valued for themselves as ends.

It follows that, at this third level, love is more than attraction, even more than collaboration; love is total, free, unconditional self-gift to the Creator and to others. Here we can choose to "lose" one focus of our being, of our existence, for another more prized one. "He who finds his life will lose it; and he who loses his life for my sake, will find it" (Mt 10:39). Here we are opened up to Love which is loss of partial self-investments, but which is gain of personal unity, integration in Christ-goals, Christ-life, Christ-love. Friendship of level two differs from the "mad love," the radical love of level three, where one gives or alienates one's own soul from oneself, abandoning it to Christ and, through Him, to others.[19]

Rare authentic love is thus possible and arrived at by means that differ from simple gratification and satisfaction of physical and social needs. Authentic love comes through suffering, through delay of gratification and finally through self-forgetfulness. This is the extreme, absolute, complete gift of an ordered self, given in its total depth, given to Truth, to Reality, to the All of *Him*, the Creator and His designs of love for us. The apostle Peter perceived this, and could write: "By *obedience to the truth* you have purified yourselves for a *genuine* love of your brothers; therefore, love one another constantly from the heart" (1 P 1:22).

Love is not only a biological crystallization of the sexual attraction or desire; the body is *not* the source of formed acts: it only furnishes material for these acts or decisions. Neither are social interactions or needs the source of formed acts. Acts happen through the *interior* of a person: impulses must be processed in the human person, in the Christian; they must be subordinated to his will, to his liberty as a child of God, a unified, integrated creature made in His own image and likeness.[20]

God is undivided. God is holocausted love. So should we be. If all loves are integrated through this third level, and, by grace, directed to God, love will be real (not merely subjective, a figment of needs and of imagination), love will be ordered and selfless; love will be *holy*.

Thus we can, through this third level, abstain from focusing on one task (e.g. physical gratification or self-expression) for the sake of another one (the Kingdom of Christ). "When such abstinence is the result of an authentic commitment to a unique mission, it is wholesome and does not cripple the personality. The sexual dimension of our life is not isolated from the whole of our existence or from other dimensions of our life. On the contrary, the orientation of our sexuality is intimately connected with the orientation of our existence as a whole."[21] Under the influence of our core value or ideal and of the third level, we can undertake a form of life which has not only a "natural disposition" in us, but which has at the same time somehow a disposition which allows us to go beyond focusing on the first or second levels only; it can move us from self-fulfillment to self-transcendence and self-transcendence for the Divine as our goal.[22]

B. Meaning of Love

At this point it may be useful to go a little deeper into the understanding of the essence of *love*. Some suggestions will have already arisen from the consideration of the different levels of psychic life. The process of love is, ideally, based on the spiritual plane (level three), on liberty and truth in our being, in our soul. Genuine love is the key to integration or unity in the person as well as among persons. Thus, if we wish to be fully persons, unified, undivided (on all three levels), we must be sure we are functioning from the "formal actuation principle of man"—not only the spiritual, but also the supernatural, the soul, the image of God—from the undividedness of love. Sex can begin in the body; love begins in the soul. Thus the qualities of the soul, of the third level, must be the elements defining love if it is to be *real* love; and real love, in turn, integrates. Hundreds of solid readings are available on the topic of love. Karol Wojtyla, now Pope John Paul II, has written a classic on *Love and Responsibility*. Jacques Maritain, noted French philosopher and very dear friend of the late Pope Paul VI, discusses love in his classic *Love and Friendship (Amore e Amicizia)*, and Aristotle also discusses love in his *Nichomachean Ethics*.[23] It is these three authors in particular that I would like to summarize, since not only do they have much in common, but more importantly they present the Christian perspective of love.

1. Concupiscence

In general, the term "love" is applied to two different experiences in the human person. On the one hand, the term "love" has been used, rather erroneously, to express a subjective experience of pleasure, of attraction, of satisfaction and well-being, of completion. This is called by Wojtyla a love of concupiscence, because it tends to find the good it is missing in the person, in another good outside the person. This type of love presupposes a limit in the person which can be eliminated by a desired object: I want you, then, as an "object," as a good for me. This does not mean wanting only in a carnal or sensual way. Carnal and sensual love may be involved (level one: self-preservation), but level two may also be operative: I want you because I am insufficient to myself, because I have need of you for my self-affirmation, for completing myself. Thus the attraction is often built on an emotional wanting; a rather intuitive pull toward pleasure or satisfaction or completion, which becomes the end. Actions are inserted into the perspective of completion, of pleasure one wishes to arrive at and pain one wishes to avoid. Persons then become *objects*, means towards personal fulfillment or pleasure, to fill up *my* life. There is generally little beyond my own self which is operative or directive: actions and interactions are self-contained in that they come in and go out from *me*, for *me*. Gratification and the fulfillment of my needs become primary. People are important insofar as they "function" in this way for me. Levels one and two are primarily operative here. Most "loves" are built to some extent on this; some "loves" are almost entirely built on this.[24]

2. Benevolent Love

There is, on the other hand, another deeper level of love, called "benevolence," or "friendship" or "true good." The love of benevolence, according to St. Thomas, is an orientation which springs from the will, from altruistic feelings for the *other*. It is a willing of good not merely for oneself, but also for the *other*, for *their* good. Whereas the "love of concupiscence" is rather subjective, idealized, "blind" as to the real characteristics or goals of the other, this "love of benevolence" is more objective, aware of the limitations of the other, and wishing the fulfillment or perfection also of the other.

Thus benevolent love is no longer primarily "I desire you as a good," but rather "I desire your good." This means dealing with the other as a *person*, not as an object that serves my personal fulfillment or perfection, no matter how good and wholesome the latter may be. Thus, the synthesis of one's tastes, interests, goals, etc. is based on what is the real good for the other, as well as for the self. The other person is considered as a *whole*, that is, on the basis of what is good for them according to the exigencies of their nature. This is a freer love than that of concupiscence, since it is freed from the subjective evaluation and spontaneous, unprocessed "choice" of the other according to the criteria of what is needed for *me*. Surrender and sharing and giving can be as a *whole* person; not a giving of body or senses only, not a giving of goals or needs to be complemented or filled; but the whole person can be given. Parts of oneself, levels of oneself, can be "sublimated" for the good of integration of the whole: sublimation is in no way the renouncement or repudiation of the principle of love; to sublimate is not to deny but to assume; it is not to destroy but to restore upon a higher level; not to condemn but to glorify. Sublimation is a peaceful effort to achieve nature's work in us, that of perpetually raising up the lower (levels one and two) by causing it to participate in the higher life (level three).[25]

Thus, real deep love and the behaviors which flow from it come from a rational consideration, a thought-out evaluation of one's own personal goals or ideals, *along with* the goals or ideals of the other as distinct from one's own, and an attempt to help the other reach those goals as a whole person.[26] Thus, whereas physical sex or caresses or intimacy may be desired *by me*, this may not be in keeping with the life-vision, the call of the other; it may not be according to the other's value system or my own, or may not correspond even to the other's need. This should be the criterion of my choice: the other's *real* good, and my own real good. Perhaps also, because of my own life-call, it may not be a "good" for me, or it could be a partial good (physiologically or socially) but not a good for me as a *whole* person with ideals (spiritually, rationally). Wojtyla puts it simply: the basis of *love* is the value of the person; the basis of utilitarianism is the value of pleasure.[27]

3. Mad or Radical Love

This benevolent love of friendship may even develop into the "mad love" spoken of by Maritain: transcendence of self to that point where I freely give all that I *am*, not merely all that I have or do, to the other.[28] Even the threefold purposes of marriage are built on this principle of three levels in a person taken as a whole; love involves offspring, fidelity and the sacrament (St. Thomas). The first end of marriage belongs to the first level of a man and a woman, as living beings: procreation, self-preservation; the sec-

ond end of marriage belongs to them as *human* beings: complementarity, social help, fulfillment, assistance, self-affirmation; the
third belongs to them as Christians, capable of self-transcendence, responsible for each other not merely as citizens here, but as
pilgrims to an eternal city.[29]

This brings us to the next question: this benevolent love, or
even this total mad-love, love which is integrated on all levels and
ordered by the third, is it what we call virtue? Up till this point we
have described mostly natural human love. "Psychic qualities,
though not guaranteeing virtue or Christian perfection, condition the normal expression or full development of them."[30] Thus,
we are saying that while this human integration, even this "mad"
love, may be available to be virtue, it is not necessarily so. When we
recognize that the order of nature, in the other and in ourselves,
originates *in God*, is guided *by Him*, and depends on Him for
existence, actions take on a new criterion for evaluation. A new
object enters in: through the third level we can begin to go beyond
ourselves to another human being, but also to a relationship with
God.

Grace works here. Grace freely given by God, liberates us
totally because it provides us with the truth of all existence: God as
the source and sustenance of my being, of love—the Alpha and
the Omega. Love of one human being for another then becomes
independent of self, independent in some way even of the other,
because it is conceived within the limits proper to a relation with
the Creator. Now there are *three ordered wills* involved: my own,
that of the other person, and the will of the Creator. The more
consistency there is among them, the deeper, freer, more stable
the love. Thus, merely human renunciation is not necessarily
virtue: renunciation may be made for my own good as a part-
person (level one, physiological) or for my own or the other's good
as a social being, as a self-fulfilling being (level two, psycho-social),
or for the general values or needs of the other as a whole person
(level three) or for God (level three). Level three, then, is the
meeting place of human and divine love. Grace works through
this level, transforming human love into virtuous love. The
person can not only respond in potency, recognizing the possible

existence of God, but can actually respond to the action of grace, with the whole self, in love. St. Augustine claimed that grace is, above all, love: "Because you have loved me first, O Lord, you have rendered me lovable." Here "lovable" has a double meaning: the person is rendered *worthy* of being loved by God (emphasis on the object, person), and also *capable* of being loved by Him (emphasis on God's action). Our reason can imagine this love of God, and our whole being can respond in love to it. This is virtuous love.

Grace, then, is a divine action which operates on the psychic structures and levels of the person, respecting freedom. Meissner claims: "Freedom is . . . a condition of the action of grace, and grace is, conversely, the condition of a person's growth in freedom."[31] Love becomes a virtue when our chosen action, on whatever level, exists in the presence of and response to God, for *His* sake. This does not exclude my own good, the good of the other, but rather raises both up to and in relation with the only objective real good, the love of God. Thus, our vocation to love as Christians and as religious, is not determined solely by the interiority or integration of our person: our need to orient our development through human love must bring us to a meeting with the objective call of the God of love.

We cannot grow in personality, in transcendent Christian love, only through our own spiritual-rational energies. The Gospels, calling us to perfection, remind us to believe in, to rely on especially, the work and truth of grace. It is *this* which introduces us into the realm of the action of God and of His love.[32] Love then becomes charity, love of God and neighbor as one: 1) to love our neighbor as Jesus does (friendship), and 2) to see Jesus in our neighbor (Mt 25:35) (mad love), and surrender to Him.[33] Mad-love for Christ is the deepest of all loves and the truest of loves, because it is eternal. It is the commandment: "Love God with all your heart, all your soul and all your strength and all your spirit" (Lk 10:27; Mt 22:37; Mk 12:28; Dt 6:5). The more radically one surrenders all one's levels to Him, the more one enters a relationship which goes beyond mere friendship and becomes more spousal; thus one approaches the goal of creation: "to see His face."

Up until now we have been presenting basic essentials. We have said that a person acts and reacts on three levels, which can be ordered and integrated hierarchically into a whole. A person interacts with these levels within himself, and also with other human beings; and both of these interactions take place in the light of the abiding Creator-within-us. Love, then, to be mature, must recognize the uniqueness of each of these persons, and of each of these specific levels and principles within persons: "To the mature person the partner is no 'object' at all; the mature person sees in the partner another subject, another human being (and as Christians we may add the other Divine Heart at work), that is, a general member of the human race; seeing him also in his very humanness (and divine-ness) . . . he even sees in the partner another specific person which means that he sees . . . uniqueness."[34] This uniqueness constitutes the personhood of a human being, and it is only love that enables one person to seize hold of another in this specific, unified way. Grasping the uniqueness of a loved one understandably results in a monogamous partnership. The partner is no longer interchangeable. Conversely, if one is not able to love in this mature manner, one winds up with promiscuity.[35]

Now, the fullest and highest kind of love is mad-love or radical love. If this total self-donation of all that one is, is made to God directly, a consecrated state results. A person is loving virtuously in charity if they love in the Heart of Christ as He loved, and if they love Him in others. Now, one cannot give oneself in total absolute depth to two people at the same time, as mentioned above: a mature love means "uniqueness," undividedness, oneness. If one wishes freely to consecrate oneself to a radical love-relationship with the Creator directly, one cannot at the same time espouse others in the same radical way; for example, one cannot give one's body or companionship or self to another in the intensity of married love. If you give all your money to one person, you cannot give all of it at the same time and in the same way to another. Furthermore, the love of charity is different from created love, even from mad-love. The object of the love of charity is of a supernatural order, the order of the Spirit; the desire to possess the loved one and to be possessed and to inebriate oneself in Him, to be loved by Him.[36]

We have dealt with the topic of love at some length now, and one may well ask what relation all this has to chastity. First of all, let us remember that a supernatural reality (love of God) cannot be built except on a corresponding human reality (love of neighbor), otherwise it would lack a base, an echo. This does not mean that the supernatural reduces itself to the earthly or mundane, but only that it must find a point of contact there, at the third level, the integrated self.[37] Where, then, is the point of contact between love and chastity? To answer this, we will next consider the notion of "purity."

III. PURITY: TO WILL ONE THING ONLY

Perhaps we can put it most concisely simply by saying:

Whoever can love
can be pure (that is, is capable of being)
Whoever can be pure
can be chaste (that is, is capable of being)

Let us define the terms: *whoever can love*—Christian love, as we have seen, is the self-gift of one person to another, a profound, free, committed respect for the other person's good as a body-soul unity loved by Jesus and desired by Him. Whether it is love of friendship or mad-radical-love, it is a choice made on the basis of transcendent values, especially the one transcendent value of God, rather than simply on the basis of needs (though not entirely exclusive of needs). The person who can love in this way can be pure.

But what does it mean to be pure? One clear element of true altruistic love, as we have seen, is the capacity to choose one good above another, and devote oneself to that good. Purity, as defined and explained by Kierkegaard, is "to will one thing only."[38] As we mentioned earlier, religion, or the choice of religious values as a form of life, expresses life *for God*, an unreserved gift of mad-love to Him. In this choice, "the truth that 'one thing necessary' (porro unum est necessarium) has assumed a concrete shape; its very existence is a witness to this word of eternal life. It glorifies God above creatures and in creatures." Religious life, then, is not only the way of closer union to God, but it is also a result of it.[39] It is a living of the "one thing only." This one thing only is a response to "Agape," the divine love which creates and raises up one universal, integrated love in us. Agape is a supernatural love, founded on the communication of divine life to the creature, drawing the creature towards divine union: "Because He first loved us and delivered Himself up for us." The goal of Agape is the blessed vision of God, being with Him.

However, though Christ brought Agape, a love superior to merely human love since it is His own, it does not absorb or suppress other loves, but "integrates them, ennobles them, enriches them, conserves them, perfects them, illuminates them."[40] Thus, human love can preserve itself and grow in supernatural love because it acquires characteristics of Agape, of Christ's love. St. Paul (1 Cor 13:4-7) names these characteristics: benignity, long-suffering, humility, service, disinterestedness, justice, truth, patience, hope, altruism, faith. In being faithful to integrated nature, and on the level of grace, a person can find salvation. In fact, true affective Christian personality integration can come about primarily through and in a love of God. "Agape is the most profound and essential mover in any affective life, as a necessary complement for an integrated vision of the person. From agape, and only from it, affectivity, virtue, every natural, legitimate love receives salvific value."[41]

IV. CHASTITY: TO WILL ONE THING ONLY IN DEED

So whoever can love in this way (Agape) can be pure, desirous of "one thing only" and can be oriented towards that "one Person only." According to our scheme, then, the person who can be *pure* can be *chaste*. Only when an individual is ready and able to seek "Him alone whom my heart loves" (Canticle of Canticles) and freely make the commitment of self as a human person to this divine Person who became incarnate, is chastity possible, and this is especially true of consecrated chastity.

A. Definition of Chastity

What is this vow of chastity? We have hinted at it earlier, and the Second Vatican Council states (P.C. n. 12):

> Chastity "for the sake of the kingdom of heaven" (Mt 19:12) which religious profess, must be esteemed an exceptional gift of grace. It uniquely frees the heart of man (cf. 1 Cor 7:32-35), so that he becomes more fervent in love for God and for all men. For this reason it is a special symbol of heavenly benefits, and for religious it is a most effective means of dedicating themselves wholeheartedly to the divine service and the works of the apostolate. Thus for all Christ's faithful, religious recall that wonderful marriage made by God, which will be fully manifested in the future age, and in which the Church has Christ for her only spouse.

Elsewhere in the same document, we read (n. 6):

> They who make profession of the evangelical counsels should seek and love above all else God who has first loved us (cf. 1 Jn 4:10).

B. Reasons for the Choice

From what the text tells us, it seems that there are two ways of looking at chastity: there is a positive element of choice, and, as for any choice, a concomitant renunciation of other possible choices. Let us look at the positive side first.

1. Christ our only Spouse

As we have already seen, a person who is pure lives in an attitude of reverence and respect for the Creator (as the one Person only), and of respect for all creatures including themselves. This means the person reveres sex and its profundity; its sublime, divinely ordered meaning as an expression of the gift of person to person, as the gift of God's unifying love.

However, as Maritain reminds us: "Whoever enters into a state of life which is dedicated directly to the radical-mad-love of God, gives to God both body and soul. The soul is given through *love*, the body through *chastity*."[42] Thus, the vow of chastity is a real holocaust of body and soul, a holocaust made as the most direct and rapid way to the perfection of charity. More precisely, it is a holocaust in that it is a correct use of sexual activity, the subordination or integration of it, in this case, to the "call from God" to value a plan of life and mission which is primary: the worship of Jesus. It is a human-Christian synthesis of self-realization through self-transcendence, an integration of all three psychic levels, ordered by the third and inspired by grace and Agape. What is this mission for which a person makes this holocaust of self? One author has put it concisely: "He who renounces matrimony confesses publicly his trust to find in God fulfillment of his needs of love; he attests with his life to treasure and to believe in the promises of the Gospel; to demonstrate in his person that eternal life is a reality which already has begun on this earth."[43]

2. For the Kingdom

Chastity places before us and before the world a living and constant sign of the *religious* dimension. Virginity, then, to be consecrated to God, must be chosen for God's sake. It is not enough that it be chosen as willed by God (I *have* to be celibate, since I chose religious life); it must be referred to Him far more directly, consecrated specifically to *Him* (Mt 19:11-12), for the Kingdom's sake.[44] Celibacy should be willingly chosen, joyfully lived as a continuous breaking of one's body, in love, for Him. It must be an organic expression or manifestation of the love, of the interior bond, of the unique intimacy between the virgin and God. Chastity is then the mastery of human values, and to live it is to master the sexual condition, to master sentimentalisms and their attractiveness, and to master them for a higher good.[45]

C. Celibacy as Choice of Value

Now, the Council documents quoted above have explicated three meanings and/or motivations of the vow of chastity. Chastity is essentially: Christological, eschatological, ecclesiological.

1. Christological

Chastity is a profound love and imitation of Christ. How? As the life of Jesus was directed toward the proclamation of the presence and the coming of the Kingdom of God in a spirit of Agape (i.e. love and service), so should we, as chaste religious, be "light" and "salt" for the world, towards the same end. This announcing or proclamation of His Father by Jesus included renunciations and misunderstandings. He renounced physical sexual gratification or intimate expression; He renounced the companionship of a "special" woman. This too is our choice (Mt 8:20; Mk 3:21, 31-35).

The Father incarnated His love for us in Jesus and now turns to us for incarnation. Jesus is the sign for us that a life wishing to consecrate itself exclusively and directly to God without earthly mediation or love is an illusion.[46] Jesus shows us how we are to be mediators, to use our "earthliness," our body, our social needs, our wills and plans of love, for the one thing only—His Father's will of love, of concern for the good of others. Christ shows us in His celibate life a way of giving ourselves totally to the Kingdom (Mt 9:12).

Jesus also shows us the meaning of faith: faith must be expressed by a free action of choice of chastity, in blindness, in pain of emptiness; a choice which my life realizes, and a witness to belief in the completion of my life by *THE* life which is God Himself, a life which comes to us through *death*, through the transcendence of Christ and of those whom He loves in this world.[47] Like St. Paul, we are called to say: "I live now not with my own life but with the life of Christ who lives in me" (Gal 2:20), and chastity is a concrete means towards this, since the flesh is "a body for Him," a body given in life and in death for the redemption of others.

2. *Eschatological*

Chastity is a reminder of our final end in eternity. It is a manifestation of faith and hope in God; a belief that in the final reality we will be taken up into God where there is "no weeping or gnashing of teeth," no emptiness or loneliness or unfulfilled desire, where there will be eternal communion and blessedness with the Father; where love will reign. This utter reliance on grace for a "new life" of faith and charity, where there is no giving and taking in marriage, in no way depreciates the present life, the human; but rather, it indicates that the religious sense or meaning is the only one to fill and condition *all* of life. Chastity thus becomes a manifestation of the grace and the constant call to transcendence. "The celibate cries out with his life to his brothers and sisters that the Kingdom of God the Father through love is awaiting its perfect realization in Christ."[48] The celibate, moreover, lives this already, here.

3. *Ecclesiological*

Finally, consecrated chastity is the sign of the Church. As the Church is the Sacrament of Christ, formed by and presenting Him, so the virgin bears this same character of the Church within: to bring Christ's chaste, pure love to the poor, the rich, the sad, the lonely. We place ourselves at the total service of the Church, in the service of redemption, in a dilated, universal love-pact, to concern ourselves "with the things of the Lord" only. As R. Schutz, prior of Taizé, speaking of virginity, puts it: "It permits one to keep one's arms open, without ever closing them, so as not to embrace only some one."[49] St. Ambrose, speaking of the maternity of the Virgin, compares the limitedness of physiological maternity to the generation of new life which is made possible through speaking, that is, speaking the word of God. This "speaking the word of God" expresses the life of the Church, of Jesus; the virgin's work, like that of Christ and of the Church, in speaking the word, nourishes and bestows divine life,[50] and can generate descendants as numerous "as the stars in the heavens," as in the promise to Abraham. Thus the consecrated virgin, always nourished and satiated above all by the word of God, becomes a living sign of the effectiveness of the word, as in Christ; of the redemptive quality of death and sacrifice, as in Christ; of the constant prayer of praise to God who does great things for us, as in Christ. Thus chastity opens us to be: for Christ, for the Word, for the Gospel (Mk 10:29). This undivided love, expressed concretely in apostolic mission, is not merely utilitarian: we do not make a vow of chastity so we can *work* more. We *do* make a vow of chastity in order that we may live more a life totally dependent on faith, in love, so that we may be a concentrated and visible sign of faith, of adhesion to the Lord, which manifests itself in an "eternal" project, an interior form of life, as well as in apostolic mission.

Let us recall, then, that "virtue" is not "virtue" if the "yes" to chastity comes about because the "no" (to physical, social, and spiritual-rational gratification) is of no value; we cannot say a real "no" to something like sex if it is considered low, evil, etc.[51]

From the positive point of view, chastity is first of all *election* or choice; a choice of one value among many, a choice of that value judged as superior and primary to others, including sex and intimate social relationships: a choice of the undivided love of Christ and of dedication to His person. In this love it is openness to all.

D. Celibacy as Renunciation—on three levels

Now let us turn to the *other* side of the coin, to the renunciation involved in the choice of celibacy. Christ says to each of us: "Sell what you have, deny yourself and come follow me." If we stop to think of it, *any* choice in life demands a renunciation. If, on the physical level, I choose to do exercise, or have sexual relations, I cannot at the same time feel relaxed. If I choose to sleep, I have to renounce doing exercise. On the psycho-social level: if I choose to be with people, I renounce solitude. So also on the third level: if I choose to make of my soul and body a consecrated, living presence of Christ, then I must obviously limit other identical expressions of love to other objects. If I choose to live my life as a "whole" person, God-oriented, I cannot allow myself to be reduced to a "part," to live only or primarily *one* aspect of my being, on one of my levels. If I want one good, I may have to sacrifice the good of another level for it. Think of the sacrifice of material goods made by St. Elizabeth or St. Jane Frances de Chantal, how they deemed nothing too high a price for the happiness of their marriage in the hour when they were faced with the death of their husbands. Yet on the other hand Elizabeth often spent hours of nights in prayer with her husband, sacrificing the physical pleasures and joys of nightly intimacy for an even greater good on another level.[52]

What do we renounce as consecrated, chaste persons? On the first level, it is to be remembered that we do not renounce our carnal being, but only the means of expression and realization of this which are false according to our chosen orientation.[53] We renounce the ecstatic joy of physical intimacy, of sexual pleasure, of any gestures symbolic of or leading to sexual union. This includes kissing, holding hands, intimate physical postures, longing or seductive looks, touching or *any* physical act representative of the specialness and uniqueness of love which belongs in our case to Jesus. However, although we do renounce sexual expression, we do not renounce sexuality: the manifestation of masculinity and femininity in their total complexity which remain beautiful and important. For example, strength, delicateness, gentleness, sensitivity, warmth and tenderness in their proper context and meaning, are particular means to be used to incarnate the tender Heart of Christ as long as they are unambiguous, clear, and restricted as such.

On the second level, the psycho-social, we renounce the intimate and faithful companionship of a beloved, the intimate complementarity of a man and a woman that brings inner security and joy in living. For example, the sharing of "secrets," of provocative discussions, of intimate presence and promises, consolations as well as mutual responsibilities. We place in the Heart of Christ our need for such attention, concern and gratification. In this way we likewise gift Christ with our wish to be a member of an intimate, circumscribed, reciprocally loving community—the family. This, of course, involves the willingness to forego the joy of seeing personal love, physically and as a personality, concretized in children. On this level the religious does not renounce every friendship, but must subordinate it and integrate it to a strict interior vigilance, to his or her "undivided love."

Finally, the third level, the spiritual-rational, offers the religious an opportunity for redemptive "death." In renouncing marriage, a spouse and children, we give to Christ our wish to be remembered in our offspring and by them. This includes also our natural wish to have our project of life furthered in them, flowering in them. How lovely it is for parents to see their children living out the ideals, the projects, the manner of good living they have lived! Likewise, we renounce personal projects of femininity or masculinity in a marital sphere; a female religious will renounce, for example, the imaginative creativity that finds joy in furnishing a home for a family and husband, in preparing a meal or social gathering, in choosing clothes and vacations together, in preparing herself most delicately for the sexual act, in ways of gratitude and intimacy during and after it. Similarly, a male religious will renounce the satisfaction of caring and providing for a wife and children, planning trips, vacations, hobbies with them, and so on. Thus, while we do not renounce our imagination or creativity, we do forego these particular precious means of expressing it. We renounce too, a faithful, unique, totally dedicated companion, a husband or a wife, for example, with whom we can share our inmost being, who can assist us in a framework of intimate love and devotion to purify our values and plans in the area of sex, and who has a special attention and thought for us. What a precious renunciation!

Renouncing sex means renouncing also a kind of self-knowledge that can come only by this interaction. Perhaps renunciations of this kind are the most difficult! A decision to live this third level for Christ gives a particular meaning to the other two. Therefore, on all three levels, we give ourselves, renouncing not only "the flesh" but also the abyss of natural aspirations in our soul and spirit; renouncing, in a word, the possibility of obtaining and willing that earthly paradise of nature: mad-love between man and woman.[54]

Sex, in openness to another, allows us in a particular way to fill part of our existential penury, be it physical solitude or the psychic incompleteness of which sexuality makes us aware. As priests and religious we renounce this type of fulfillment.[55]

All in all, we can see then, as John Paul II put it: "Some think that the virtue of chastity has a purely negative character. Chastity in this view is one long 'no.' Whereas it is above all the 'yes' of which certain 'no's' are the consequence."[56]

Furthermore, as we mentioned earlier, a manner of sexual behavior which consists in abstaining from genital, intimate, unique contact, is normal psychologically if it is chosen freely, for valid rational reasons and if it respects the highest good of the person.[57] Supernaturally this psychological normality can be virtue if it is chosen as a fundamental option, a call to mad-love, radical love in Christ and for Him, and if it is lived clearly, deeply, totally and stably, in a mature, integrated person. It is a true holocaust, a gift of body and soul, and only a profound and daily living and experience of faith and of love can maintain an equilibrium between the positive value of chastity and the negative aspects of renunciation so as to facilitate a fertile and holy chastity, a fertile and holy love.

E. Virtues included in Chastity

When we take the vow of chastity, we also automatically commit ourselves to the practice of a number of other virtues inherent in the *living out* of the holocaust. These include:

1. First Level (though based on the third level: will)

i. Modesty: Modesty emerges from our interiority, from the desire to keep values and facts within, especially the value of sex. It is an attempt to control the tendency to dissimulate the sensual and sexual values of the body without considering the value of the whole person and his/her life goal. Modesty, in other words a careful, willed, delicate quietness as regards clothes, body (e.g. eyes) and actions, bespeaks a message to others of mature humanness, uplifted, as "inviolability," as John Paul II calls it. "Do not touch me, even by your interior desires"[58] (this is similar to Christ saying, after His Resurrection, "Do not detain me."). I belong to Jesus and these are His, to be used for the work of the Father. This modesty, of course, implies continence, that is, abstinence from use of the genitals or any part of body-existence leading to sex.

ii. Temperance: It is the temperate or sober person who possesses self-mastery; in such a person, passions do not take precedence over reason, or over will. Wojtyla claims that this is indispensable for human maturity.[59] In controlling sense pleasures, we maintain senses in their proper perspective in the Divine Plan of nature. As Rahner puts it: "There is necessary a wise and sober 'self-control.' "[60]

2. Second Level: related virtues

i. Justice: "Blessed are they who hunger and thirst for justice's sake, for they shall be satisfied" (Mt 5:6). Justice is the fundamental principle of the existence of the person and of the Church. It is based on a respect for obedience to the order of nature, the value of the whole person in Christ. It is recognizing the rights of God and the rights of the person according to the plan of God for him. In the plan for our vocation and of that of others, it is recognizing and revering what *God* plans in our life and respecting that, not asking that for which we have no right.[61]

ii. Simplicity, sincerity, honesty, humility: Chastity presupposes a basic crystal-clear capacity to lay oneself open to the Creator and say, "*You* are Lord, *You* are Creator, all I am and have is yours." This is the truth, the simple truth. It is simplicity, and purity. It is accepting that truth (honesty) and surrendering oneself to it, without any attempt to take back by rationalization.

3. Third Level: related virtues

i. Faith: trust in the person of Christ and in His promises; trust in the word of the Creator, in His covenant of love with us. Trusting that His love is profound, that it purifies us, sanctifies us, raises us up if we cooperate with it. The simple prayer of John Paul I expresses this faith: "Take me Lord, as I am, with my defects, with my limitations, but make me become as you desire me to be."[62] We ask Him to make of our incompleteness, the incompleteness of a physical love, a redemptive and eternal love.

ii. Fidelity: Chastity is a radical fidelity to the great commandment to "love the Lord, your God, with your whole heart and mind and soul, and your neighbor as yourself " for the love of God (Mt 19:19; 1 Cor 7). This commitment of self to a radical living of the commandment of love is made, knowing that the choice is a decision for an incalculable and uncontrollable future. It is made with a faith in the power of the Cross. It is a promise of fidelity to God's plan in our human nature, His plan in our soul. Rahner says: "That which was received as grace must be again merited in fidelity, in the same manner that the sexual impulse must become love, which without fidelity, in fact, without fidelity conquered with great fatigue, is not yet love." One remains faithful because the call of eternal life and the love of God, of the confession of the Cross of Christ precisely in this way needs to be realized in our lives.[63]

iii. Prudence: This virtue is based on the concept that the value of the person must be seen according to the moral good that he accomplishes in his life. The truly prudent person will make the effort to evaluate all things, every situation, every relationship, every movement of the heart or body or will, according to the moral good. This central point of moral good is one's realization in Jesus Christ. For us as religious, it is our realization in spousal love, an undivided love of Jesus, with no division in our psychic levels which predispose us to this. Am I prudent? Do I live evaluating the consequences of my friendship for myself, for others, for the Church? Am I responsible for my actions? Is this relationship, this love I seek to realize, serving the *real* good of the whole person or only an apparent, part-good, because of my needs or theirs? Does it serve as a means to salvation which Christ and the Church want for us?

Since we have reviewed the natural bases for chastity, along with the supernatural core and the meaning of the vow, it seems opportune now to review some of the problems that can arise regarding the actual living of the vow.

V. USES AND ABUSES OF CHASTITY

We have said that consecrated virginity, or chastity, is an efficacious mobilization of the spiritual and natural energies of the person, for the "one thing necessary": union with God in love of Him and His creatures. While the highest natural perfection of the person can come about by an integration and hierarchic ordering of the psychic levels of the person in mad-radical love for another human being, there is *another* supreme perfection, incomparably higher because it is of a different order: the supernatural mad-radical love of God for men and women, and of men and women for God.[64] The former human love, symbolizing the second type of perfect love of God and His spouse, is vividly recalled in the beautiful Canticle of Canticles. Keeping this as a supernatural vision of our ideal as celibates consecrated to God, let us now look concretely into our levels of existence and the manner of living our vow on these levels. Keeping in mind the principles for mature love, for purity, for chastity, already proposed, we can see that problems in chastity arise when one does not succeed in integrating one's sexuality into one's total dynamics as a person. Integration fails when one closes oneself off to one level, in narcissism, solitude, egoism, thus lacking in real love towards oneself, towards God. What renders an act sinful or limited is the distortion it causes in the totality of the person, in the concrete design, human-supernatural, of God for that creature.[65] Thus, chastity's goal is to bring human nature to perfection in love: for religious, in the radical love of God. Freedom of heart means the release from egoism, in an integrated psyche that seeks God alone.

St. Ambrose discusses the difficulties living a life of chastity presents, and he considers in particular the difficulties it presents for women. He especially underlines particular characteristics and desires of women which give rise to such difficulties: the desire to have the gift of a spouse, to be "special"; the desire to be needed, remembered; the desire to be fecund, for children; the need to talk, to converse, to communicate; the need for security, for support; fear of solitude in life; a sentiment of sympathy, mercy for others, sensitivity. All of these needs tend to dispose women to more ample, vast, deep human relationships.[66] How can such needs as these be dealt with when one has taken a vow of chastity? Could there be a search for compensation? Indulgence? Let us try to understand what happens, or what *could* happen "but for the grace of God."

A. First Level Uses and Abuses of Chastity

1. On the psycho-physiological level, *masturbation* may become a problem. This genital self-stimulation produces pleasures, excitement, fullness, desire, warmth. The gravity of the act depends on the level of distortion of our nature: a difference should be made between an isolated *act* of masturbation and a habit or pattern of masturbation. How is masturbation a distortion? It is allowing the first level of our psychic being to gain ascendency over the other two, especially over the third; it is a search for

pleasure from oneself, an egoistic, narcissistic, immature stance toward being. Now, the Church teaches that masturbation is grave matter (Document on Sexual Ethics). Therefore, given sufficient knowledge and consent it can also be a grave sin. In any case, it is not something to be taken lightly. If a habit has been established, serious attempts should be made to overcome it (e.g. psychological help).[67]

Masturbation for an adult is a disorder. It is generally a manifestation of unintegrated non-sexual needs which underlie the sexual symbolization. In fact, scientific research indicates that for 17% of women and for 23% of men, sex in itself is the problem.[68] Masturbation may occur because of anger, fear, hurt, sadness, failures, or when another need is not gratified. For example, when a need for dependency is not gratified, the person may, in anger and fear, seek gratification from themselves. Generally people who masturbate regularly can be found to have difficulties in interpersonal relationships, in communicating, in trusting, in regulating time, interest and concern for others, in being or feeling accepted.

The problem of masturbation *may* have some source in the environment, but it is generally already a problem *within the person*, intra-psychically; the person has not yet learned how to be aware of and handle other needs which arise within. If one knows one's needs and the values of one's vocation, and yet chooses, because of some inconsistencies of needs with the values (especially if they are already conscious), to please oneself by this stimulation, the seriousness of the offense increases; the will of level three is used here for a value which is not the "greater good." As von Hildebrand puts it: "The attachment to a good and the desire to possess it is the more unselfish (or selfish) in proportion to the depth and nobility of that good,"[69] in other words in proportion to the level in the hierarchy of values and to the correspondence to grace within us. When we are *really* possessing the superior good, attachment to the inferior (physical) seems ridiculous and outgrown.

2. Another problem on the physical level can arise either between a man and a woman, or between two men or two women.

This is *heterosexual or homosexual physical involvement*. As indicated earlier when dealing with "renunciations," a radical integrated love of God above all, and of one's neighbor in Him, in the religious life precludes any intimate physical expression, whether that be hand-holding, kissing, or caressing. Such interaction between man-woman, woman-woman, or man-man, on an intimate plane, has sexual connotation, no matter *what* rationalizations are offered, or in what close situations one finds oneself. No man religious or woman religious has a *right* to ask another to engage in such practices since they are objectively contrary to one's plan in life: undivided integrated love for Christ. Reasons such as "helping to overcome inhibitions," "learning to trust," "I need you," "I need to relax," "gratitude," "sympathy," and so on, are rationalizations since all these "needs" can be satisfied in another way, with means which are in keeping with the promise of life one has made.

Self-actualization is not our goal; self-transcendence is. Such actions use the other as object, not as person: they deny, remove from others that third human level and the level of grace which should be most operative in them in their specific vocation. The same can be said of actions which involve the senses such as the eyes: "looks of lust" often mentioned by authors, prolonged looks of intensity, depth, seductiveness, searching, penetrating. The unconscious message of sexual desire is clear if both are honest enough to recognize it. These too should be avoided. Christ looked on the woman with *love*, not with sexual desire, and she got the undivided message clearly. He told her to *go* and sin no more (Jn 8:11); He did *not* say: "*Come* now and sin no more"! A good concrete criterion for evaluation can be: whatever act I engage in with the other "in secret," would I be comfortable doing the same thing with him or her in the community room or refectory, or among my community? Or at least, would it be objectively acceptable as such? The ultimate criterion, of course, is the degree of honest self-transcendent love of God that I am willing to live.

3. A third way in which one can be dominated by the first level instead of living as integrated on all three levels, is to get caught in *body-worship*. This can have two facets. There are those who worship the body "curing it to death"! They exercise it to the point of

exhaustion, take pills to the point of becoming internalized drug stores; live on the scale for fear that a half ounce gain might appear; dress especially to reveal its sexual beauty and youth; color their hair to change what God is doing in them and to impress and attract; sleep to excess, so as to avoid bags under the eyes. This can be body-egoism: has such a body been given to Jesus for Him to do with as He wills? The other extreme can also creep in: a sister or a priest cares nothing about her or his body. She or he eats until her femininity or his masculinity is unrecognizable, or dresses like the local house-maid's maid or bartender; or refuses to take an aspirin or cold tablet at any cost; is afraid to see her/his body in the mirror. Nor is such body-worship an exclusively feminine preoccupation; both men and women can well ask themselves if their way of looking after the body is indeed a way of preserving it for God's service, is indeed a way of praising the Creator for the integrated gift of sexuality.

4. A final way we can consider here is the possibility of reducing one's ability to love by isolating the physiological level through seeking pleasure in *sexual novels, movies, magazines, television shows, and the like*. Not that, should such matters turn up when one is reading for other goals (classics in literature, for example), there is need to discard these; that would be prudishness, and just as much a distortion of chastity. What is in question here is making a "diet" of romances, with all their details and graphic descriptions and stimulating presentations; thus living a life of sexual pleasure vicariously, letting the other do it, but seeking to participate in its effects. I wonder if we should not see the majority of soap operas in this light? Do these *really* relax us, uplift us, help us praise God freely for the gift of sexuality? If so, then why the *drive* not to miss one day: "*my* program" is on! Is there not an egoistic pleasure there? Do we go that eagerly to chapel?

B. Second Level (Psycho-Social) Uses and Abuses of Chastity

We move on now to consider the affective interaction between friends or colleagues. The psycho-social level can open us up to concretize our love for God by expressing it in cooperation in the life-plan of our brothers or sisters in community, and of others engaged in similar Christian works and goals, by sharing plans as well as genuine affection and support.

Wojtyla warns in his book, that while affection is necessary in relationships, the affective life should not become the driving force of our existence. It should not degenerate to the sensual, but be integrated into a plan of love, love for the whole complex human person, in the Lord.

This brings us to the topic of *friendship*: a particular type of psycho-social affective relationship which is not only permissible, but also encouraged as a genuine means of concretization of the love of God in us, of self-transcendence. True friendship will indeed provide opportunities for transcendence, since in recognizing each other's limitations one is asked to love in spite of them and above all even when self-gratification is not forthcoming because of them.

Chastity can be supported by affectivity if it is used to support values, the values of the person in his/her plan of spiritual life. This will mean that a person who tends to sensuality will have to change that sensuality and affectivity into love, by continence, by virtue, by reflection. What is affectivity? It is the desire for the presence of another human being. It need not be only physical presence, though it can regress to that. Now, just as there can be an egoism of the senses (we have just described how; at level one, values can be subjectivized to pleasure, physical sensations, sensuality), so also there can be an egoism of sentiments, of affectivity.[70] This is not a body-sentiment, but rather a psychological, psychic one. Here one can use the other to satisfy not bodily needs (though it may regress to that), but affective needs, such as needs for affection, support, understanding, concern.

This attitude of egoism can be seen in an underlying subjective self-concern: nobody loves me, nobody cares about me, you didn't visit me yesterday, or tell me where you were going, or send me a card, and so on. Thus one begins to give love and attention and concern in order to be assured that in time of trouble one will get back the same. I write you a letter, you should write back; if not, then forget it, you are of no *use* to me. Never *said*! But done! I give you a gift, and expect one back; if not: "You never think of me as much as I do of you!" Are we seeking affective pleasure in others? Staying in our small groups because we feel "comfortable," in other words because we are afraid to feel insecurity or uncertainty, afraid to *really* love? If that is the case, then we are using our group of friends for ourselves, for our comfort.

This can be *apparent* altruism. I appreciate others' pleasure only because it enhances my own; I sift it through my own affective needs, and take out what I need, and forget the person! Thus, for example, I will be happy only when they try something I am interested in, undertake a project like mine. I do not mean we should not be pleased at this. A "real genuine good" gives deep joy when we see others pursuing it, too. If I know that interest in spiritual reading is good, then I am happy when another begins to read more spiritual books. But the joy is not because they are reading them so as to be like *me*, but reading them so as to grow into *Jesus* whom perhaps by His grace I have radiated.

Love, real love or friendship should not be mutual egoism, a fusion of pleasures where both get what they can from each other for their own affective needs and feed off the "community" for the same. Support is necessary, even some gratification of affective needs is useful for spiritual growth. But the question is: which needs, how much, and what values?[71] Affective support for such needs as nurturance (care for others) or domination (ordering, controlling), when in the service of values such as the Kingdom of God or charity, can be a blessing for a religious and one of the gifts of community living. On the other hand, affective support for needs such as dependency or aggression and values such as power or possessiveness do not help religious to be the "servants of the Lord" they have vowed to be. The vow of chastity excludes sensible affectivity which could lead to marriage. Other sensible affectivity, as long as it is not equivocal, should be considered openly and honestly in all its depth with regard to possible underlying motivation.[72] Affectivity, just as sensuality or sensitivity, even when highly developed in an individual, can open a person to a deeper, more alive and profound surrender in love to Jesus, or close a person in more securely on self. It can be a means or it can become an end in itself.

On the other hand, just as insensitivity to sex does not equal chastity, nor even provide a favorable environment for that virtue, so also for lack of affectivity. A person who is cold, dull, aloof, will have a hard time of it to cooperate with vitality and joy in building up the Kingdom. We need affective friendships too, warm, delicate, deep. But we need to integrate them and order them hierarchically in the levels of our being. And without continence, the natural energies of sensuality and those of affectivity will become "material" for egoism of the senses or eventually for that of the sentiments.[73] In other words, without self-control, freedom in loving is impossible.

At this point it may be helpful to list some criteria for evaluating friendships: woman-woman, man-man, and man-woman friendships. There should be the following:

1) Love of solitude, and a desire to remain in solitude (no fear of being alone).
2) Love of one's project for life, freely chosen for Jesus.
3) Desiring the good of the other person; being willing to leave them if need be.
4) Deep sense of honesty not to falsify or allow the relationship to degenerate.
5) Interior freedom, having one's heart where it should be, doing what one promised.
6) Greater commitment to and love of prayer, intimacy with Christ (not necessarily only a *felt* difference).
7) Relationship accepted, not sought for with anxious impatience, not indispensable for affective maturation.
8) Freely chosen and pursued, not manipulated, harassed, seduced into.
9) Includes warmth, but avoids behavior typical of engaged, dating or married people (carnal, sensual, corporal, tactile).
10) Lived in poverty.
11) No intimacy and sentimentality of an affective type expressed in prolonged visits, dates, useless correspondence, indefinite conversation, personal and regular costly gifts.

12) Respect for intimacy of the other: not *needing* to participate in secrets, such as, for example, to know the psychological needs of the other and the deepest core of their personality; yet able to *accept* such secrets *if* the other wishes to share them and if it is helpful.

13) Avoids passion, romantic love disguised as spirituality.

14) Non-exclusive friendship, which does not impede one's mission and availability to others and to the Kingdom, but in fact fosters these.

15) Carefully chosen friendship, not entered into haphazardly, but evaluated: its limits and its good are seen.

16) Tried friendship: with good will it remains faithful in times of joy and in times of difficulty; does not arise only from prosperity, but also from trials.

17) Acceptance: compassion in realizing one another's limits, suffering in this, but correcting and challenging one another.

18) Complementarity or agreement: not necessarily wanting or thinking the same way, but understanding and respecting, foreseeing necessities of the other; forgetful of self.

19) Trust: respect for the presence of God in the other, being optimistic as regards our friend growing in good, but realistic also in their struggles to live out that good.

20) Openness: truth is an absolute which is greater than friendship. A friend worthy of the name will sacrifice personal pleasure for the spiritual good of a friend, and be truthful with them.

21) Moderation between involvement and detachment: God asks me to sanctify the world by my involvement in every endeavor, also with friends; but also by means of discipline and detachment.[74]

Friendship, then, as St. Augustine summarizes it, is a union among persons who love God with their whole heart and love one another, and are united for all eternity to each other and to Christ Himself.[75] Friendship is a stepping-stone to perfection which is essentially love of God and of one's neighbor, in such a way that a person, out of friendship with another person, enters more fully and entirely into friendship with God.[76]

A quick word here should be said regarding another abuse of this second level. There are some who, unwittingly, engage in playing with the affections or feelings of others. They create in others the illusion that they care very much for them, and give rise to the expectation of great personal concern and affection without any intention of pursuing the relationship. The relationship is left in a state of ambiguity, compliments are given as a sign of affection, but interest is quickly withdrawn once it is clear that someone else's affection can be obtained. On the other side of the coin are those who play with the emotions of others by making them feel guilty, or put-down, or useless by harsh, aggressive, grandiose remarks. There are those also in-between: they are your friends as long as you serve their esteem. For example, they will say to someone who is interested in a topic such as music: "Oh yes, we are very proud of Sister So-and-so, who is our musician!", yet they will be the first to criticize her among other friends, or to ask that she be changed. These are affectively arid people, indifferent to the problems of others, with difficulty in human relations, spurred on by domination and a need to compensate for the renunciations of chastity which are felt as frustrations, by means of their fickleness, domination and radical independence. There is an emptiness of personality within. All these are not ways of a chaste love, but of an egoistic love, of a grandiose caricature not only of the Heart of Jesus, but even of a mature human being.

C. Third Level (Spiritual-Rational) Uses and Abuses of Chastity

True chaste love can regress from this level to a preponderance of one or both of the other two levels, as we have seen. On this level, however, a few abuses are also possible.
1. If love and chastity imply involvement for the Kingdom, service should be a natural result of that love: the wish to be for others as Jesus was, as exemplified in His washing the feet of the disciples. Often egoism creeps in: altruistic, self-transcendent ideals get cramped into the little box of "I," "mine," "me": *my* projects, *my*

ideas, *my* creativity, are the most important, the others can run up a tree. Is this the love of a compassionate Christ who reached down to heal, to console, to minister? Is this the meaning of His Incarnation?

2. There may also be those who live in a world of ideas, incapable of feeling. They have made of their precious femininity or masculinity a crystallized show-piece, or a bitter herb. Reasoning always, detached, critical, alone, they claim they are self-controlled, and would never "lower themselves" to love anyone but themselves. And yet, how fast these "intellectual values" can go out the window when someone of the opposite sex appears on the scene to complement their narcissism further! Is this the spontaneous, involved, universally vulnerable love of the Heart of Christ, the Spouse?

3. Finally, even values and declared spiritual ideals of love, community life, spiritual life, can be used for egoistic ends. We *must* have a spiritual director, because we are unable to get along with the sisters or brethren (escape). We must have a friend, because the others are naive, don't understand, aren't up to our thinking (need for affection and support). We can even use love itself (and our manifestation of it in service and warmth) to bolster our own pride: how good I am, not like the rest of them! How subtle we are! Although Christ called the Pharisees whited sepulchres, He never insisted that *He* was the paragon of perfection: "Be perfect as your heavenly Father is perfect."

No doubt the list of abuses of chastity could go on, and on. However, it will profit more for each of us to choose one or two (or three) of the points which are most relevant to our own personal failures in living a chaste love, and to reflect and work on these.

VI. MEANS TO GROW IN CHASTE, CELIBATE LOVE

What are some of the means we can use to help this treasure of chaste, celibate love grow? Love is a gift, but also a conquest. It is formed by the work of the person in the light of his nature and will, as we have seen: it is enlivened by grace, by the work of the Spirit within us. What can we do, on our side, to be available to grace? Most of the means which we will discuss for renewal of our vow of chastity can be applied also to deepening our religious commitment in general.[77] We can make, however, particular application of these means to our religious love, to our chastity.

A. Asceticism-Discipline

By now it is quite clear, from what has been presented earlier, that, in order to arrive at a living, chaste, consecrated love, it is indispensable that we work to overcome in all its forms the subjectivizing of our values, all our egoistic trends. This means that there is necessary a strengthening of our will, an integration of the different levels of our psychic life in the service of the will to love. In order to objectivize the value again, to see love and chastity the way Christ sees them, the way Christ works in our lives, we need to open our interior life and seek *truth*, to bring ourselves into line with Christ's request for us and our promise to Him.

John Paul II clearly poses for us a need for renunciation of one value in order to grow to a higher one.[78] This means, as mentioned already, that every choice for the predominance of one level (not its exclusiveness) involves a renunciation on another level. Whoever wants to have *all* love is so frustrated in the seeking, that they can never freely decide nor give themselves to any love. Self-fulfillment is a dead end. Only self-transcendence can allow us to find "Him whom our heart seeks" in all situations. Paul VI spoke of the asceticism needed for maturation of the personality: "The young candidates for the priesthood should convince themselves that they are not able to follow their difficult way without a special type of asceticism more demanding than that which is asked of all the other faithful . . . It will be a demanding asceticism, but not a suffocating one, which consists in the deliberate and assiduous practice of those virtues which make a man a priest: self-denial in the highest degree—an essential condition if one would follow Christ (Mt 16:24; Jn 12:25), humil-

ity . . . obedience . . . prudence, justice, courage and temperance . . . responsibility, fidelity . . . detachment . . . poverty . . .
service."[79] Rahner puts it similarly, pinpointing this renunciation
in celibacy: "He who makes of his celibacy an act of love, forgets
himself, and this is possible by the freeing grace of God . . . he
possesses happiness and finds that perfect joy that he only has,
who knows how to cry serenely"; "Without faith, without the
acceptance of the incomprehensible folly of the cross, without the
hope against every hope, without the blind obedience of Abraham and without prayer, one does not go on" (in celibacy).[80]

For those looking for new experiences, it may be good to
remember that "also responsibility, the mystery, the acceptance of
pain and renunciation make for experience."[81] In renouncing a
great intimate human help, for Divine Love, we place our trust
more firmly and directly in God's grace. What greater experience
than that of being grace-filled, grace-integrated? Renunciation by
our free choice can be acceptable to God and profitable for growth
in love only if He fills that void which has been left; only if we do
not allow other compensations to creep in.

"How easy it is," says von Hildebrand, "for the man who has
renounced the delicious, liberating happiness of the highest
earthly partnership, to fall into pettiness and attachment to lower
goods . . . turn wholly to bitterness, unemancipated. How often we
attempt by distractions or routine, or by a lazy drifting on the
stream of superficial experiences to shirk the cross which God has
sent us."[82] The parable of the great supper (Lk 14:16-21) reminds
us that the freer the heart from egoistic or material ties, the more
undividedly it can concern itself with the things of God. Thus,
death is necessary; renunciation, decision, are necessary for integration, for the holocaust of an ordered love which seeks one
thing only.

B. Prayer-Meditation

Following from this renunciation there is the need to follow
the words of St. Paul: "Be watchful, stand firm in your faith, be
courageous, be strong" (1 Cor 16:13) through the means of

prayer. Maritain claims the best way to advance in virtue is through contemplation: the mad-radical-love of God expressed in open contemplation in the contemplative life, or in the masked contemplation of the active life.[83] This means living a life based on the Gospels. Rahner, speaking of means or sources of celibacy, says: "One believes *first* in the Gospels, and one lives believing with undaunted courage that the Gospels know truly that which makes sense."[84] We need to meditate on the Gospels if we are to know them, and to abandon ourselves to the Gospels if we are to learn to live love as Jesus did. Thus, Paul VI urges priests to use the supernatural means: "Christ's priest will receive new strength and joy daily as he deepens in his meditation and prayer the motives for his gift and the conviction that he has chosen the better part. He will ask humbly and perseveringly for the grace of fidelity, never denied to those who ask it sincerely."[85] There is no better way than devotion to the Eucharist to fill our cup to over-flowing with His love.

C. Loneliness and Solitude

Group experiences are necessary; they are also an expression of chastity and a means of deepening it. However, solitude and loneliness are *first of all* indispensable if one is to find oneself, integrate those aspects and levels of self which are troublesome, and have an identity, a *personal* identity in Christ which can be offered in gift to others. Desert experiences lead a person into contact with the basic essential needs, values, attitudes of the self, confront a person with them, and give time to work through a proper stable integration. We need the silence of solitude to be with our Spouse, to find the hurt and fears and uncertainty and pain, as well as the joy and peace and desire and gratitude, so as to offer Him our lamp filled with oil, not some empty substitute.

D. Community Life

Perfectae Caritatis (n. 12) recalls to our minds that "chastity is practiced with greater security, where a real sense of community flourishes upon the genuine brotherly love reciprocated by all of the members." The community can offer to each religious selfless interest in his or her plans, concern for the person, a sense of belonging, of worth, of solidarity in a love-plan which is theirs too, a sense of security. As David Stanley says: "These sincere over-tures (of brotherly or sisterly involvement) certainly spring from no natural source, but have their origin in the love God has shown us in Christ Jesus Our Lord (Rm 8:39)."[86]

If there are weaknesses in the vow of chastity, in friendships among our fellow religious, would it not do us good to look into our community living? Have we supported and loved and called forth the heart of another, or have we rather criticized, alienated, competed with them? Community involvement, interest in others' lives *for pure love*, is the best antidote to self-cultivation. Community living is a fruitful field for renunciation, but it should not be *only* that. We *need* support of positive values and of neutral, vocationally consistent needs. We are incomplete: no one is an island! We need God's love in our sisters or brothers as example, as unction, as peace, as challenge.

E. Examen

An honest evaluation of our needs, our egoistic trends and the needs which are dissonant with love, is helpful. Can we define the need, and integrate it with our values? Here the examination of conscience is most useful. (See Appendix at the end of this chapter.)

F. Service

Finally, service is a genuine way of renewing, preserving and augmenting one's love; service is a way of bringing the fruits of solitude back, to try them in reality. We can easily live in an "imagined" love of Christ in solitude, until the door-bell rings, or someone calls for help from the kitchen or the sacristy, etc., and our "ideals" go down the drain. "Why me again?"

Love knows no boundaries, even to death on the cross. Service is love in action. Can we not only *wait* to be assigned a task, but be so vibrant with expectant love as to *find* those situations where Christ can serve and love again in me, and "wash their feet"? And do it with tenderness, with love?

So we have arrived, or rather, we have just begun. *Living* our vow of chastity is something serious, deep and challenging. We *can* and should seek to respond to that challenge and in a renewed way, to love chastely as Christ loves, to surrender our body, our social and spiritual needs to intimacy, to Him, to His Heart; to enter into His love, to open and abandon ourselves to it, and humbly to carry that precious diamond in our being, so that He may be reflected joyously in every facet of our virginal daily gift to those He has gifted us with, in service, in mature, pure and chaste love.

Love

> Who create life, and give life,
>   Create me again today in your love.
> O God, Love infinitely dear,
>   Gift me to live for you.
> O God, infinitely faithful,
>   Help me in every tribulation.
> Love, infinitely good,
>   Act in my every action.
> Love, infinitely sweet,
>   Do not abandon me ever.

Saint Gertrude

Appendix: Is our love virtue?
Here are some questions we can ask ourselves, some criteria we can follow

1) *Affirmation of the Value of the Person*

Does my love, my interaction with others, respect all three levels of the person? Or is it merely emotional, satisfying my need to avoid loneliness, or my need for power, or for exhibitionism? Am I using the person? Do I keep in mind the spiritual life and the values of the person, the perfection of their soul, and not merely the gratification of my or their bodily or social needs? Can I put the other person's needs before mine, their values alongside my own? Can I love the other person when they are not fostering my own needs but *are* fostering my values? Virtue is built by *will* (as well as by emotion); the pull here is towards values rather than towards needs.

Does my love stably respect the other's ideal of life, their means of reaching that goal; does my love support the other in the pursuit of this goal and help discern its objectivity? If the other's chosen goal is destroying them, for example, through indiscriminate gratification of needs and uprooting of values, will I have the courage to tell them about my concern and discuss it with them? Can I risk their anger for an objective stance I take, for *principle*?

2) Reciprocal Participation of Persons

The essence of love is most profound in the mutual free gift of self. A person can only *freely* renounce his right to be independent and inalienable, master of oneself, for a higher good (for God in the religious life). Do I try to impose my "love" on another by possessive questions: "Where have you been?" "Whom do you prefer?" "Why didn't you tell *me*?" Do I push to tell another *how* they should love me, *when* and *how much*? Do I use "devices" to "con" them into loving me: making them feel guilty, playing the victim, offering gifts? Do I ask them if they love *me* more or do I work with them to see if they have grown more in loving God, in loving others? Do I *invite* them or manipulate them?

Are we both loving each other for God, with emotion, warmth, tenderness, as well as with objectivity, with reason? Is our love a reciprocal gift and mutual partaking of two *persons*, not merely two bodies; the presence of two *souls*, not merely two persons? Is my union with the other on the level of sense, or the affective level, for pleasure or social needs especially? (This is egoism).

Do I know how to accept as well as to give, always creating an interior climate of respect for the *person*, for the animating, searching soul?

3) *Choice and Responsibility*

Love is built on freedom and responsibility, which presupposes a capacity for individual introspection and discernment. Each one should take responsibility for himself or herself in the love relationship, and feel responsible also for the good of the other. Can I make decisions on my own, apart from the other, according to the values I have been called to by God? If I am wrong, can I be honest in admitting my error and asking forgiveness, taking every possible means to grow in deeper values? Will the other respect my choices even when not benefiting directly from them? Can I similarly respect the other's? If our form of friendship or love is not compatible with religious life (or chosen vocation), what choice will I make? Leading a double life? Renouncing higher values? Renouncing the relationship, but taking it out on someone else? Do I always push off the blame for difficulties in the relationship, or with others, onto the *other*? (That is a lack of mature responsibility). What am I looking for most in this love?

4) *The Commitment of Freedom*

Freedom is a property of the will; the will tends towards good. It is, then, the nature of the will to *seek* and *choose* the good which corresponds to its nature. In the light of this, how free am I to be open to myself; am I always defensive of the particular good I have chosen (physical, social)? Am I *stable* in seeking an absolute good, an infinite good, the good of the soul above all things? Do I orient my time to seek and to serve especially the spiritual needs of my friend? Do I often or generally feel resentful that my time is not my own, that I am asked to do things which I do not like? Do I feel "free" only when I am doing what I *like* to do, and orient my life to this? Now that I am up in years, do I think I deserve more materially, more time, more consideration, more benefits, more love and attention? Am I sufficiently free interiorly to regulate my time and my energies to serve others in a radical way and continuously for Christ? Can I detach myself from that involvement which is destructive of the organizing principle of my life, of Christ's love-relation in my life? Am I wishy-washy in my dependability: loving and happy and warm one day, but aggressive, putting down, distant the next? When I see the major "good" or value of Christ clearly, can I pursue it, even if it means losing the "love" and esteem of another?

> Adapted from Karol Wojtyla [John Paul II]
> *Love and Responsibility*, (London: Collins,
> Fount Paperbacks, 1982).

Readings on Chastity

Vatican II on Christian Virginity: *LG* 42c, d; *LG* 43a, 44a, 44c; *PC* 12a; *OT* 10a, b; *PC* 16a, b.

Renunciation for the Kingdom: Mt 8:20; Mk 3:21, 31-35; Lk 14:26; Mt 10:37; Lk 18:29; Mk 10:29; Mt 19:29.

Meaning of Chastity: (Christological, Eschatological, Ecclesiological) *PC* 5; Mk 10:29 (for Him); Mt 9:12 (for the Kingdom); Mk 10:25; Mt 19:12; 1 Cor 7:32; Mt 19:11-12; 1 Cor 7:7; *LG* 44.

Magna Carta of Virginity: 1 Cor 7.

Genuine love based on truth: 1 Peter 1:22-23.

Footnotes

1. Patrick Hart (Ed.), *Thomas Merton, Monk*, (New York: Image Books: Doubleday & Co., 1976), p. 15; and in Thomas Merton, *Contemplation in a World of Action*, (New York: Image Books, 1973).
2. Adrian Van Kaam, "Sex and Existence" in *Sexuality and Identity*, Ed. by M. Ruitenbeck, (New York: Delta Books, 1970), p. 126.
3. Jacques Maritain, *Amore e Amicizia*, (Brescia: Morcelliana, 1978), p. 15.
4. Karol Wojtyla (John Paul II), *Love and Responsibility*. (London: Collins, Fount Books, 1982), pp. 104-109.
5. Ibid., pp. 104-105.

6. Philomena Agudo, *Affirming the Human and the Holy*, (Whitinsville, Mass.: Affirmation Books, 1979).
7. Dietrich von Hildebrand, *In Defense of Purity*, (Chicago: Franciscan Herald Press, 1970, reprint of 1930 ed.), pp. 1-7.
8. Wojtyla, pp. 88-95.
9. Ibid., pp. 90-91.
10. Ibid., p. 47.
11. Ibid., p. 112.
12. Ibid., p. 110.
13. Maritain, p. 12.
14. Ibid., pp. 14-18.
15. Wojtyla, p. 167.
16. Victor Frankl, *The Unheard Cry for Meaning*, (New York: Simon and Schuster, 1978), pp. 80-81.
17. Wojtyla, pp. 54-57. (The spirit cannot follow the same principles as the body.)
18. Angela Romano, *L'amicizia nell'itinerario vocazionale della vita religiosa*, (Rome: Rogate, 1977), pp. 39-40.
19. Maritain, p. 28.
20. Wojtyla, pp. 49-50, 54 ff.
21. Van Kaam, pp. 132-133.
22. Wojtyla, p. 255. (See, for example, the lives of St. Augustine and Charles de Foucauld).
23. Wojtyla, pp. 80-82, 40-44; Maritain, *op. cit.*; Aristotle, *Nichomachean Ethics*, VIII, IX.
24. Jean Guitton, *Human Love*, (Chicago: Franciscan Herald Press, 1966), p. 9.
25. Wojtyla, p. 83; Maritain, pp. 18-19.
26. Wojtyla, pp. 40-44.
27. Ibid., p. 31; also pp. 30ff.
28. Maritain, pp. 30ff.
29. Von Hildebrand, p. 27. Cf. also B. Lonergan, "Finality, Love, Marriage," in *Collection*, Ed. by F.E. Crowe, (London: Darton, Longman & Todd, 1967), pp. 16-53.
30. Romano, p. 66.
31. W.W. Meissner, *Foundations for a Psychology of Grace*, (Glen Rock, N.J.: Paulist Press, 1966). Quoted also in L.M. Rulla, *Depth Psychology and Vocation*, (Rome: Gregorian University Press, 1981). The citation from St. Augustine and its interpretation are taken from Rulla, p. 168.
32. Wojtyla, p. 40.
33. Maritain, p. 34.
34. Frankl, p. 81.
35. Maritain, pp. 19-24.
36. Edward Schillebeeckx, *Il Celibato nel Ministero Ecclesiastico*, (Rome, 1968); see also: *Celibato per il Regno*, Proietti et al, (Rome: Ancora), pp. 269-270.
37. L.M. Rulla, *Depth Psychology and Vocation*; also L.M. Rulla, J. Ridick, F. Imoda, *Entering and Leaving Vocation: Intrapsychic Dynamics*, (Rome: Gregorian University Press, 1981) and Rulla, Ridick, Imoda, *Psychological Structure and Vocation: a study of the motivations for entering and leaving vocation*, (Dublin: Villa Books, 1979). These books deal with the question of consistency and inconsistency among a person's needs, values and attitudes, both conscious and unconscious.

38. Soren Kierkegaard, *Purity of Heart is to Will One Thing*, (New York: Harper and Row, 1970).
39. Von Hildebrand, p. 127.
40. Romano, pp. 63-65.
41. Ibid., p. 67. (See also the questions for self-examination on pp. 46-48).
42. Maritain, p. 56.
43. Yves Raguin, *Celibacy for Our Times*, (Wheathampstead, Hertfordshire: Anthony Clarke Books, 1978), pp. 47, 51, 90, 99, 111, 119.
44. Von Hildebrand, p. 93.
45. G. Perico, "Spunti per la lettura della Dichiarazione su alcune questioni di etica sessuale," *L'Osservatore Romano*, March 6, 1976, 5.
46. Jose Rovira, "La Dimensione Teologico-Morale in una Vita di Celibato per il Regno," in Proietti, et al., *Il Celibato per il Regno*, (Milan: Ancora, 1977). Rovira refers to other authors: S. Villato, "Redonner sens au celibat religieux?" *VC* 43, 1971, 146, 148; B. Besret, *Liberation de l'homme*, (Paris, 1970), p. 83.
47. Karl Rahner, *Lettera Aperta Sul Celibato*, (Brescia: Queriniana, 1967), p. 31.
48. Bruno Proietti, "La scelta celibataria alla luce della S. Scrittura," in Proietti, et al., p. 74. See also the bibliography of this book: pp. 275-278. Also: Schillebeeckx, pp. 120-126; J. Aubry, "Al seguito di Cristo," in *Per una Presenza Viva dei Religiosi nella Chiesa e nel Mondo*, (Torino-Leumann: A. Favale, 1970; 2nd Ed.) pp. 450-454.
49. Ibid., p. 74. Also in J. Aubry, p. 452.
50. St. Ambrose, *De Virginitate*, I, 4, 14; I, 6, 30. See also: Vittorino Grossi, "La Virginità negli Scritti dei Padri. La sintesi di S. Ambrogio: gli aspetti cristologici, antropologici, ecclesiali," in Proietti, et al, pp. 153 ff.
51. Marc Oraison, *Il Celibato: Aspetti negativi e realtà positive*. (Turin: Borla, 1967), Ch. III, pp. 46, 94.
52. Von Hildebrand, p. 122.
53. Romano, p. 38.
54. Maritain, p. 55.
55. Rovira, p. 259.
56. Wojtyla, p. 170.
57. Rovira, p. 260.
58. Wojtyla, pp. 174-186.
59. Ibid., pp. 166-173; also John Paul I, *The Theological Virtues*, and John Paul II, *The Cardinal Virtues*, (Rome: La Parola, 1978), pp. 30 ff.
60. Rahner, p. 26.
61. Wojtyla, p. 245-249.
62. John Paul I, p. 11.
63. Rahner, pp. 24-25.
64. John Paul II, pp. 21-23.
65. Maritain, pp. 54f.
66. Rovira, p. 262. Also Wojtyla, p. 166 and Maritain, *passim*.
67. For a good reference on Masturbation see Bernard Tyrell, "Masturbation and the Sexual Celibate," *Review for Religious*, 1976. A very balanced approach can also be had in: J.J. Farraher, "Masturbation," in the *New Catholic Encyclopedia*, 1967, Vol. IX, pp. 438-440.
68. Rulla, Ridick, Imoda, Unpublished research. Chicago/Rome.
69. Von Hildebrand, p. 119.

70. Rovira, p. 282.
71. Rulla, pp. 127 ff.; also Rulla, et al., passim.
72. Von Hildebrand, p. 120.
73. Wojtyla, pp. 153-158.
74. Nn. 1-14 from: Rovira, pp. 305-306; nn. 15-18 from: Aelred de Rievaulx, *L'Amicizia Spirituale*, ed. P. Gasperotto, (Siena: Cantagalli, 1960), p. 77; nn. 19-20 from: St. Augustine, *De Civitate Dei* 19, 8; *PL* 41.
75. C. Browning, "Religious and Love. A New Dimension," *Review for Religious*, 1968, 27, 636. Also, J. Galot, "Responses aux questions sur les Conseils Evangeliques: les Conseils Evangeliques et l'Engagement dans le Royaume," *Forma Gregis*, 1969, 2, 132-133.
76. Adrian van Kaam, *On Being Involved: The Rhythm of Involvement and Detachment in Human Life*, (Denville, N.J.: Dimension Books, 1970).
77. A.C. Hughes, *Preparing for Church Ministry: A Practical Guide to Spiritual Formation*, (Denville, N.J.: Dimension Books, 1979), p. 86.
78. Wojtyla, pp. 194-200.
79. Paul VI, *Sacerdotalis Caelibatus*, Rome, 1967.
80. Rahner, pp. 14 and 26.
81. Ibid., p. 30.
82. Von Hildebrand, p. 123.
83. Maritain, p. 32.
84. Rahner, p. 29.
85. Paul VI, p. 25.
86. D. Stanley, *Faith and Religious Life: A New Testament Perspective*, (New York: Paulist Press, 1971).

Bibliography

St. Aelred de Rievaulx, *L'Amicizia Spirituale* (Spiritual Friendship). Ed. P. Gasperotto, Siena: Cantagalli, 1960.

Agudo, Philomena, *Affirming the Human and the Holy*. Whitinsville, Mass.: Affirmation Books, 1979.

St. Ambrose, *Virginità*. Rome: Citta Nuova Editrice, 1974.

Aristotle, *Nichomachean Ethics*. Books VIII, IX.

Aubry, J., *Virginità e L'Amore*. Turin: L.D.C., 1980.

St. Augustine, *De Civitate Dei* 19,8; *PL* 41.

Canadian Religious Conference, Series *Donum Dei* no. 6, 16: Celibacy; no. 15, Maturity (1973).

Conner, Paul, (O.P.), Friendship between Consecrated Men and Women?, *Review for Religious*. 1981, 40, 5, 645-659.

Cusson, Gilles, (S.J.), Chasteté Consacrée—Vie sexuelle et affective. In: *Quaderni, C.I.S.* VII—Spiritualità Ignaziana, 1972-73. Rome, pp. 145-156.

Flannery, Austin, (O.P.) (Ed.) *Vatican Council II: The Conciliar and Post Conciliar Documents.* Northport, N.Y.: Costello Publishing Co., Inc., 1975.
— Decree on the renewal of religious life (Perfectae Caritatis), pp. 611-680;
— Decree on the training of priests (Optatam Totius), pp. 707-724;
— Decree on the ministry and life of priests (Presbyterorum Ordinis), pp. 863-902.

Farraher, J.J. Masturbation, *New Catholic Encyclopedia.* 1967, Vol. IX, pp. 438-40.

Frankl, Victor, *The Unheard Cry for Meaning.* N.Y.: Simon and Schuster, 1978, pp. 80-87.

Galot, Jean, (S.J.), La motivation Evangelique du Celibat. In: *Gregorianum.* 1972, 53, 731-757.

————, *Teologia del Sacerdozio.* Firenze: Ed. Fiorentina, 1981; pp. 246-267.

Guitton, Jean, *Human Love.* Chicago: Franciscan Herald Press, 1966.

Hart, Patrick (Ed.), *Thomas Merton, Monk.* New York: Doubleday and Company, 1976, p. 15.

Hughes, A.C., *Preparing for Church Ministry. A practical guide to Spiritual Formation.* Denville, N.J.: Dimension Books, 1979. Chapters: Expanding the Life of Charity, pp. 43-53; Consecrating Sexual Love, pp. 76-86.

John Paul I, *The Theological Virtues.* Rome: La Parola, 1978.

John Paul II, (Karol Wojtyla) Audiences of March 11, 18, 24, 31, April 7 to May 12, 1982. Bollettino, Pontificia Commissione per le Comunicazioni Sociali. Vatican City, 1982. (All are on Continence for the Kingdom).

————, *The Cardinal Virtues.* Rome: La Parola, 1978.

_____, *Love and Responsibility*. (Trans. H.T. Willets) Collins, Fount Paperbacks, 1982.

_____, *Prayer of the Holy Father John Paul II on the Occasion of Holy Thursday, 1982*. Vatican Polyglot Press, March 25, 1982, pp. 10 ff.

_____, *Sign of Contradiction*. London and Worcester, Great Britain: St. Paul Publications, 1979. Relevant: pp. 127-135; 197-206.

Knight, David M. *Cloud by Day, Fire by Night*. Vol. I: Chastity. Denville, N.J.: Dimension Books, 1981.

Lewis, C.S. *The Four Loves*. Glasgow: Collins, 1981 (1960), pp. 107-128.

Lonergan, B.J.F., (S.J.), Finality, Love and Marriage, in *Collection: Papers by Bernard Lonergan, S.J.* (Ed.) F.E. Crowe, S.J. London: Darton, Longman & Todd, 1967.

Maritain, J., *Amore e Amicizia*. Brescia: Morcelliana, 1978 (1963).

Merton, Thomas, (O.C.S.O.), *Love and Living*. New York: Farrar, Straus, Giroux, 1979. Solitude and illusions, pp. 22-24; Love and needs, pp. 32-34; Levels, p. 34; Obstacles to love, p. 36; Symbols, p. 68.

_____, *New Seeds of Contemplation*. New York: New Directions Publ. Corp., 1972 (1962). (Contemplation as necessary for love).

_____, *Contemplation in a World of Action*. New York: Image Books, 1973. Contemplation in a World of Action. Ch. IX; The Identity Crisis, Ch. III.; Renewal and Discipline, Ch. V.

_____, *No Man Is an Island*. Garden City, New York: Image Books, 1955.

Nuttin, Joseph, *Psychoanalysis and Personality*. New York: Mentor Omega Books, 1962. The Three Levels: pp. 220 ff.

Paul VI, *The Celibacy of the Priest*. (Sacerdotalis Caelibatus). No. 604. Huntington, Ind.: Our Sunday Visitor, 1967. (Rome: June 24, 1967).

————, *Evangelica Testificatio*. Second Part A 13-15, 39, 42-48.

Proietti, Bruno, Triacca, A. *et al. Celibato per il Regno*. Milan: Ancora, 1977.

Raguin, Yves, (S.J.), *Celibacy for Our Times*. Edward Malatesta, (Ed.). Wheathampstead, Hertfordshire: Anthony Clarke Books, 1978 (1975).

Rahner, Karl, (S.J.), *Lettera aperta sul Celibato*. Brescia: Queriniana, 1967.

Romano, Angela. *L'amicizia nell'itinerario vocazionale della vita religiosa*. Rome: Rogate, 1977.

Rulla, L.M., (S.J.), *Depth Psychology and Vocation: a psycho-social perspective*. Gregorian University Press, Rome; Loyola University Press, Chicago, 1971.

Rulla, L.M., (S.J.), Sr. Joyce Ridick, (S.S.C.), F. Imoda, (S.J.), *Entering and Leaving Vocation: intrapsychic dynamics*. Gregorian University Press, Rome; Loyola University Press, Chicago; 1976. (Deals with consistencies and inconsistencies which influence the living out of such values as chastity).

————, *Psychological Structure and Vocation: a study of the motivations for entering and leaving the religious life*. Villa Books, Dublin, 1979. (A shorter version of the 1976 book above).

Sacred Congregation for Catholic Education. *A Guide to Formation in Priestly Celibacy*. Rome, 1974. (Cf. Nos. 47-52; asceticism, Nos. 53-57; underlying problems, Nos. 57-58; Friendships, Nos. 59-61; guidelines for sex education, Nos. 40-46.)

Sacred Congregation of the Doctrine of Faith. *Declaration on Some Questions of Sexual Ethics*. Rome, 1976.

Stanley, David, (S.J.), *Faith and Religious Life. A New Testament Perspective*. New York: Paulist Press, 1971.

Tettamanzi, D. *La Virginità per il Regno*. Milan: Edizioni O.R. 1982.

Tillard, Jean Marie Roger, *Davanti a Dio e Per Il Mondo*. (Before God and For the World). Rome: Ed. Paoline, 1975, pp. 152-160.

Tyrell, Bernard, Masturbation and the Sexual Celibate, *Review for Religious*. 1976.

Van Kaam, Adrian, (C.S.Sp.), Sex and Existence. In H.M. Rivtenbeck (Ed.). *Sexuality and Identity*. New York: Delta Books, 1970, pp. 123-144.

_____, *On Being Involved*. Denville, New Jersey: Dimension Books, 1970.

_____, *The Vowed Life*. Denville, N.J.: Dimension Books, 1968, pp. 169-175, 186-206, 213-215, 240-241, 292-297.

Von Hildebrand, Dietrich, *Man and Woman*. Chicago: Franciscan Herald Press, 1966, pp. 58-74.

_____, *In Defense of Purity*. Chicago: Franciscan Herald Press, 1970 (1930).

_____, *Celibacy and the Crisis of Faith*. Chicago: Franciscan Herald Press, 1971.

The Way. Supplement 10, 1970. Entire issue on Chastity.

CHAPTER III

OBEDIENCE

"Thy will be done . . ."

I. INTRODUCTION

> "Take O Lord, and receive my entire life:
> my memory,
> my understanding,
> my whole will.
> All that I am and all I possess
> you have given to me.
> I surrender it all to you
> to be disposed of
> according to your will.
> Give me only your love and your grace,
> With these I will be rich enough
> and will desire nothing more."
>
> *St. Ignatius*

The essence of what is to be said here about obedience is contained in this profound prayer of St. Ignatius. We can repeat these words with devotion, with pain, with gratitude, or perhaps just automatically! It is in order to deepen our understanding of each phrase, to increase the intensity of our zeal in pronouncing each word, that we come now to consider the vowed life of obedience. What follows here will aim towards integrating some essential theological insights with basic psychological realities in order to aid us in the perfecting of our promise of full self-surrender.

II. DEFINING HUMAN ELEMENTS IN OBEDIENCE: LEVELS OF BEING

In order to have a global vision of religious obedience as we did with the other two vows of poverty and chastity, it seems necessary again, first of all, to understand the essential, basic elements and processes in the normal human personality. These are the foundations and basic material for the living out of the counsel of obedience. Obedience exists in us as human beings on three levels: 1) the psycho-physiological; 2) the psycho-social; 3) the spiritual-rational.[1] We act on all three levels at any given moment, though one level may and can be more prominent than others at times. Each of these levels has its own "inherent" potentialities and natural "laws" of obedience. These work together and are necessary to predispose us to the supernatural workings of grace.

A. Psycho-Physiological Level [2]

We live on a physiological level. We are complex human organisms with biological, chemical processes. These are innate processes which occur independent of our knowing, though the effects of them will be experienced by us consciously, e.g. we do not consciously feel the change in chemical compounds, yet the feeling of hunger comes to awareness as a sign of a need which is below conscious awareness—tissue depletion.[3] Where does "obedience" fit in here? On this very human level, obedience is a mere reactive condition—physiological laws implanted in us by the mind of the all-loving Creator function automatically, as long as there is no disease or abnormality physiologically involved. Our body obeys the psychic request for satisfaction of the bodily need: when the blood slows down, the muscles tighten, the eyelids begin to sink, one stretches out for a pleasant respite of sleep. When the water level is reduced, the body signals a feeling of thirst with a reaction of enjoying a cool glass of 7-Up, water, or a warm cup of coffee. And all these functions of the body work together. There is a natural law, in a sense, which derives from a "somatic or bodily integration" even here, i.e.: "The integration of the body includes not only the . . . static total of the mutually coordinated limbs and organs but also the ability to react correctly, 'normally,' and insofar as it is necessary, efficiently. All this is contained in the notion of somatic integration—and is seen exteriorly in the bodily constitution, and what we consider the 'whole statics and dynamics of the human body.' "4

Emotions may result from these bodily processes and dynamics. However, emotions are NOT somatic reactions (e.g. the chemical imbalance or expectancy) but psychical events which of their nature are qualitatively different from the reaction of the body itself.5 Physically and psychically, because of the physiological needs, we feel some way—more or less good or bad, depending on whether or not the natural, innate "laws" are fulfilled: e.g. I am internally depleted of water; I feel weak; I feel thirsty; I manage to transcend my fatigue, get my limbs together, and get to the water fountain—or if I dislike water, I may take 7-Up; I drink; I feel better. Thus, each cell of the body must be healthy, alive, functioning, so that every member of the body—every organ, limb, tissue, etc., may function well, so that the entire body may be healthy. This is law. This is nature. At times, in fact, even on this physiological level, one part may sacrifice itself for the universal good of the entire body; e.g. after a heavy meal the blood rushes to the stomach for digestive purposes, leaving other parts of the body less effective: e.g. one may not concentrate as well, or run as well, or be as alert as earlier. Or, on sustaining an injury or infection, other parts of the body will rally to the rescue of the affected spot by working more to produce blood cells or corpuscles necessary to alleviate the situation. What a beautiful automatic system of innate laws: laws all ordered toward a final, overall good, the healthy functioning of the physiological self. The successful integration of the parts for the sake of the whole involves each part being adaptable to function more or less, as is necessary, to keep the whole body functioning at its best. And all this without our even being aware of it.

If the message or signal sent out by the body is misinterpreted or ignored: e.g. if the weakness from lack of water is believed by us to be caused by a need for sleep, and one retires; it will not really help the restoration of the body to its optimal, total functioning in the service of life, since the source of the trouble is the need for water and not the lack of sleep; so one will wake up still feeling weak. Similarly, if one does not like the taste of cod liver oil when it has been recommended, and does not take it, balance is not restored.

Thus, even on a physiological level, we are obeying: tissues obey cells, limbs obey tissues, etc. We obey the laws of nature in our physiological being: we sleep for the goal of life and alertness—we give up consciousness in sleep for the greater good of the whole body and being. In hundreds of ways each day we are obeying, even without our consciousness, sacrificing ourselves for a greater good—even physically—for the end of our physiological being: efficient functioning, life. Here we might even recall our submission to the laws of nature, of body, through the years—our reactivity to age: grey hair, sagging features, or slowing down of movement, a faltering uncertainty in walking, etc. Then there is death itself—a law in nature. "In death, man is asked to even 'give up' or detach himself from the laws of physical nature itself." As Rahner says: "In death, man is really asked in the most fundamental manner whether he will allow himself to be disposed beyond himself into what is hidden and incalculable, and he thereby renounces himself."[6] At least on this level, the law of death is stronger than the law of life, and the body renounces itself. How obedient our body is, even without our awareness, even unto the end!

B. Psycho-Social Level

On the second dimension of our existence or living, we expand or transcend our own bodily existence and needs (which occur rather automatically) to include the deeper level of existence where we give meaning to the world outside ourselves, and not merely react to the sensuousness, the emotivity of the meaning of the non-conscious world within our bodies. This level could be called the level of our life of social relationships, i.e. our lived relationships with the world of people. It presumes, of course, that the person we are is developed to the point that it can supersede the merely physiological aspects in us, and open us up to the need for others, to sensitivity to others. Here one needs to feel whole not merely physiologically, i.e. assimilating and accommodating to one's environment merely in a bodily way, but there also emerges a thirst for meaning beyond these bodily needs—needs for social recognition, esteem, care, concern. "Man assimilates his environment not only at the biochemical and physiological level, but also as a (more conscious) 'meaningful situation,' "[7] and this meaning is found not merely in an expanded awareness of *self* with more potentialities, but in an expanded awareness of the meaning of self in relation to others. Thus, even when feeling alone, there is an implied absence of relation to another. Thus we come to live constantly with meaning derived from relationship with others.

What about obedience, even on this natural level? Now, just as the proper functioning of the parts of our physical being is necessary for the effective integration of the whole, and this implies following innate laws, so there is a similar process on this level, too. Let us look at how this takes place.

We are social beings; social interactions are as necessary as is food, for our completion, for our growth. This means there is need for forming friendships, forming a community. There must be a diversity of specializations for progress of the community, so that each member may grow through the diversity and richness of the other. Otherwise the other or community would be redundant; we would be sufficient to ourselves if all were similar or equal.

Here laws of obedience come to be seen. Labourdette writes:

> Obedience is born from a fundamental necessity of the human person to be social . . .; [it means] . . . to fight against my will insofar as it manifests itself as individualistic, closed, turned in on itself. Rather than isolating oneself and leaving oneself out of community, which means 'death' to this part of the social being, one must personalize oneself ever more, discovering 'time in and time out,' ever more freely, and with more clarity, that the person does not exist nor realize himself unless stabilizing valid relations with others and inserting himself there where the community is.[8]

Thus a natural obedience occurs as one strives to move away from individuality and physiological concern with personal life and automatic goals of satiation, survival and growth towards a widened version of fulfillment with and through others as persons.

We then obey, or concede to, not only these natural physiological and social tendencies, but also we obey by putting limits to our own concerns for self alone, being willing ourselves to belong to a social group and community, to collaborate in it, under the guide of constituted authority, also, for the common good of the group. Then a new goal beyond ourselves is formed: the common good. The end of the group then is to assure the development of the common good, since it is the good of all who belong to the group.[9] Obedience consists in sensitivity and response to the necessities and requests of others, renunciation of one's own desires and interests at times for a greater good. For example, members of a family come mutually to obey, i.e., respond to each other's needs for the common unity and joy and growth of the family. It is the same for a chosen social environment, such as friendship or associations of one kind or other. Friendship, or membership in any group, being for the common good, presupposes justice, i.e., an obedience or submission of one's own vitality to that of the greater group goal or end.[10] Authority and rules are established either spontaneously and mutually, as in democratic organizations, or naturally as in the family hierarchic structure. Thus, because we have innate social needs, we come to obey those rules which both foster our own rights for growth as an individual and at the same time the good of the entire body of members. In some way obedience is materially and spiritually utilitarian on this level.

As on the first level, however, to reach the necessary goals, obedience to common rules may require a certain transcendence or certain renunciations on the part of the individual. For example, husbands renounce their own individual desires or interests in order to work, to care for, to cooperate with the wife, in obedience to the law of love for wife, for children. Wives forget their own fatigue, or hurt or insecurity; they obey the desires or needs or tendencies of the husband or children for their own mature growth and happiness. Renunciation of immediate desires for the sake of the family, employer, community or state is a transcendence of ourselves, a going beyond our own self-interests in obedience to a higher common good. This transcendence enlightens us as to our latent characteristics and challenges us towards growth and further fulfillment. Self-transcendence reveals those characteristics within ourselves which otherwise would forever remain hidden. What facilitates this movement from level one into level two? The answer takes us to level three: our spiritual-rational potential.

C. Spiritual-Rational Level

What is involved in this level? Within our being there is the capacity and tendency to transcend the limits of immediate facts and the material process (as chemical interaction, social presence or absence, etc.). Prescinding from these immediate experiences of the first and second levels only, we are able to come to some evaluation of existence or being as such. Through our reason and intelligence we can come to know and experience moral obligation, to judge situations as good or bad rationally (not merely as emotionally appraised),[11] not merely in reference to the here-and-now, to personal gratification or fulfillment, but we are able even to transcend the limits of our own situation here-and-now for principles beyond ourselves: for reasons of "goodness, of beauty, of truth," etc. in themselves. This level allows us to go beyond a particular stimulus, beyond the process of our life "which is materially enclosed" and determined in itself.[12]

This level allows us to obey in a truly human fashion. We can judge meaningful situations as relevant to our own and others' good, for the here-and-now, and specifically *beyond* the here-and-now. We can even prescind from the material benefits which may accrue to us in the here-and-now, so as to be for truth, for good, for being, beyond ourselves. On this level the object of obedience goes beyond obedience to the laws of physical nature and obedience to the common good, the fulfillment of self along with others. Here there is obedience to truth, to principle for its own sake.

Our spiritual-rational level makes possible an obedience which involves conscience—judgment, decision, and action according to objective norms or principles beyond oneself. Whereas level one alone may indicate to us that we are thirsty and hungry and need liquid and food, on level three we can choose what to eat and drink and the circumstances of our dining. Rather than eating immediately to fulfill our physical needs we may postpone our dining in order to share the enjoyment of it with family and friends.

On level three we come to obey our whole self: the "I" which transcends any one part of myself, and can also obey truth, i.e. even transcend all of myself for a greater objective good, obeying an object beyond myself for reasons beyond myself. This allows a kind of obedience to situations or experiences which may hurt by renunciation on one or both of the first two levels, but which has meaning on a logical level of truth or the ultimate good which is perceived at the third level. A maturer, more profoundly human obedience is possible here, since we are freer—to obey not merely reactively, nor in a utilitarian way according to one's own or another's human needs only, but also for the sake of principles in themselves.

Also, through this level, one's choice not to obey on one level may be an obedience on a higher level. For example, though fatigued, one may spend a while with a friend, assisting them, rather than sleeping. Though a friend may need help, one may spend the time preparing something for the common good of all. If one is asked to obey and it is against the principle of truth or justice (e.g. in a totalitarian regime), one chooses not to obey—this is not disobedience but obedience on a higher level. This is a delicate issue and we will take this up later under "Uses and Abuses." At times this obedience will require pain—renunciations of gratifications or obedience on the other levels. Yet this level frees us most to be what we truly are, human in the deepest sense of the word.

John Paul II writes: "The freedom appropriate to the human being, the person's freedom resulting from the will, exhibits itself as identical with self-determination, with that experiential most complete and fundamental organ of man's autonomous being."[13] Differing levels of emotion issuing from needs on the first or second levels are integrated under and with and by the emotion resulting from the third level—the pull toward objective good, and in particular, towards moral good or away from moral evil.[14] It is the third level that allows the most complete obedience, because it facilitates the human integration that is necessary for a more perfect (complete) human obedience. John Paul II states: "Integration is the manifestation and simultaneously the realization of unity on the basis of the multifarious complexity of man ... It is complementary to transcendence."[15] Because the consciousness of level three takes precedence over feelings, it generally brings with it an order or subordination of levels which is the condition of self-determination, self-governance, self-possession. It is a truly free, objective obedience based on the realization of the *total* personal dynamism. It includes not only the capacity to be subjective and know and determine itself from within (internal rules), but also the capacity to accommodate itself to reality and external truth by reasoning (external rules)—in other words, the capacity to be objective. A mature human obedience requires the integration of both subjectivity, knowing my reactions, and objectivity, forming my actions.

One essential point to be made here, before we move on, is this: "It is in the transcendence [going beyond emotivity] and not

[only] in the integration of human emotivity itself that the deepest meaning of the spirituality of the person is manifested; and it is there that we find the most adequate basis for asserting the spirituality of the human soul."[16] Our natural transformation under the action of the values we experience, prefigures, prepares and predisposes us in a way and continues to assist the supernatural transformation which it is meant to serve.[17]

III. DEFINING THEOLOGICAL ELEMENTS IN OBEDIENCE

A. Christian Obedience

Up until now we have examined obedience on a human level. Obedience, to be *Christian*, must first be *human*. We are rational beings, endowed with intelligence and free will, and therefore can understand and freely choose to order our lives in an obedient fashion.[18] It becomes Christian obedience when it acknowledges an entirely transcendent reality that is truly worthy of our absolute loyalty. Although Jesus did say "Render to Caesar that which is Caesar's," i.e. live a human obedience, He added "and to God that which is God's" (Mk 12:17). This is of another nature. John Paul II, in his encyclical *Dives in Misericordia*, puts it clearly: ". . . man cannot be manifested in the full dignity of his nature without reference—not only on the level of concepts but also in an integrally existential way—to God. Man and man's lofty calling are revealed in Christ through the revelation of the mystery of the Father and His love."[19] And how is the mystery of God our Father revealed to us? Through grace, first infused in us on the day of our Baptism.

What is grace? Grace is a supernatural gift enabling us to follow the singular, unique way of realization of God's love in imitation of Christ. It is God, reaching our hearts in loving initiative, building an alliance of love with us: "I will be your God and you will be my people" (Lv 26:12). Jesus Himself fulfills His part of the alliance through the most total form of obedience imaginable—with "an existence impregnated with the Will of the Father"[20] unto death. "The Word I say is not mine" (Jn 7:16). "If I say I do not know the Father I would be like you, a liar" (Jn 8:55). "The Son cannot do anything of Himself, but only that which He sees done by the Father" (Jn 5:19). "I have come down from heaven not to do my will, but the will of Him who sent me" (Jn 6:38). "I come, O Lord, to do your will" (Heb 10:7). Thus God reaches our hearts through the gift of grace and calls us to cooperate in His love-pact. "And I will put my spirit within you and cause you to live by my commandments, and to keep my judgments and do them. And you shall dwell in the land which I gave to your fathers; and you shall be my people and I shall be your God. And so I will deliver you from all your impurities" (Ezk 36:27-29; cf. Ezk 11:19-20).

Thus God takes us into His Heart and becomes more intimate to ourselves than our innermost being: *"intimior, intimo meo,"* as St. Augustine says. He establishes Himself in a collaboration, a mutual obedience of love in an indwelling in us; not a collaboration, however, of an equal level, as some sort of equal partnership, for His contribution is far, even infinitely more, in excess of ours. We now come to be sons and daughters, thinking of our existence not as God and us standing next to each other, but within each other. We are surrounded, enveloped by His life, since grace is a life *in* God.[21] All is His and He is ours. Our humanness, on all our levels, becomes His. His plans are ours and ours are directed to Him. We obey Him.

Now, at this point one may think of this "supernatural" grace as super-human or non-human. While it is of another nature, it does not destroy the human values (including the natural values of obedience), or throw them into the background. On the contrary, human values and elements take on a new meaning and worth.[22] Obedience takes on a particular higher meaning—it remains our action, but it is at the same time, now God's gift, enlightened by faith and directed to Him. How does this happen in obedience concretely?

Rahner explains obedience as having two dimensions: functional and religious. Obedience is "functional" if it is a will to obey to maintain order, to facilitate interdependence, to foster a common will of society for one's own good and fulfillment and for that of society, i.e. to make things run smoothly. There is no ideology or value existent behind this. Human development or existence is primary. Actualization and fulfillment are its goals; self-transcendence is a means.

In religious obedience, however, all that is human is encompassed in faith. Every act of submission or acceptance is seen as oriented not merely toward man, but toward God, in His providential design of love for the world. Whereas functional obedience is a submission to events, especially for one's own sake, religious obedience is a response to God's love: it is the interpretation of events which changes.[23] The Covenant, for Jesus as for us, then, is the commitment of a life entirely given to actualize not merely ourselves, but above all, the designs of God in saving the world and ourselves. In seeking the "part" assigned to us by God, we are obeying as Christians. Christian obedience, then, is "the realization of the project of God in the human person"; therefore, it is a full valuing of ourselves—a freeing and liberation of ourselves and our projects and obediences which were merely within the confines of the human level—it collects all the human plans and puts them into the perspective of the infinite plan of God for us.[24] It brings us to an obedience and measure of ourselves which is transcendent—goes beyond the confines of the human vision and human integration and human "functioning" only.

Christian obedience, then, differs from human obedience since it is built on a different value system: a) the presence of the will of the Father and the designs of Providence, rather than the will of a human being only; and b) a vision of oneself as neither master of one's own destiny nor slave to the limitations of oneself or others. In Christian obedience there is a vision of self as son or daughter engulfed and enlivened by a love which heals, transcends, and wishes to respond in obediential love to the covenant invitation. Grace then enables us to obey "beyond" mere human reason for mere human retribution or order: e.g. "If someone gives you a slap, turn the other cheek; if someone takes your tunic, give him your mantle; if anyone orders you to go one mile, go two miles with him" (Mt 5:39-41). Obedience is based now on another law, the law of Christ which is His living word (Gal 6:2; 1 Cor 9:21). It is a law of liberty (Jm 2:12; 1 P 2:16; 2 P 2:19) because it is the law of the Spirit of life (Rm 8:2). Brother Rueda, Superior General of the Marist Brothers, summarizes it well:

> The Christian existence is an existential answer to the love with which the Father loved us in Jesus Christ and in His Church. This existential response consists, on the one hand, in an interior love which continues to grow and mature unto its fullness, and, on the other hand, in a gift of self to others in the acts of every day under the sign of the holy will of the Father in the service of His Kingdom, and for the fulfillment of the history of salvation.[25]

Therefore, Christian obedience can be looked at in a broad sense as a free acceptance of all that is necessary, which we concretely cannot avoid—the inevitable, because it is part of the disposition of God, part of the hidden charity in His mysterious plan of love for us. In a *strict* sense, Christian obedience is adherence to legitimate authority which bends our wills in particular precepts, in concrete situations.[26]

Now, how is submission to the plan of God's love for us, for our salvation, seen in the "transformed" levels of our existence, through the eyes of grace?

On level one, the psycho-physiological, we believe in the care and sustenance of the body not merely for its own fulfillment or proper functioning, nor to avoid pain, nor for personal goals such as physical achievement, health, etc. Rather, as Christians, we submit to the laws of nature (at first more automatically, later rationally) believing them as a transfiguring process in the divine plan of our perfection and salvation.[27] Death itself, the ultimate obedience, and our submission to it, is a gesture of faith in eternal life; death being authorized and effected by a loving God as a call to the final transformation in Him.[28]

On level two, Christian obedience, through faith in Jesus,

transforms our natural submission to all legitimate authority into a filial submission to an eternal, loving Father. All authority is seen as being derived from Him who created the universe and rules it.[29] "Whoever welcomes the one I send, welcomes me; and whoever welcomes me, welcomes the One who sent me" (Jn 13:20). Going beyond the "common good" as goal, or social fulfillment as goal, Christian obedience on this level is summarized beautifully by Hinnebusch:

> . . . if we are all one in the Holy Spirit, each one still retains his own individual distinctive personality, and therefore in charity we must reverence everyone as an individual person and love him as such, and will that each be his own true self, the self that God's creative love and providence intends that he be. Our love for him, working in the likeness of God's creative love, labors to bring each of our brethren to his own true perfection . . .
> [It is] labor to keep one another develop[ed] in accordance with each one's true God-given potentialities.[30]

Thus Christian obedience on this level is a filial expression of living the commandment: "Love God, and your neighbor as yourself for the love of God." Obedience to others becomes a reflection and expression of obedience to the Father, our Creator.[31]

One's own self-concept also changes here, from being necessary for others in a complementary, equal, human way for mutual development, to seeing oneself as an emissary, a light of His love sent to others to bespeak His love:

> You yourselves are our letter of introduction . . . a letter coming from Christ, given to us to deliver, written not in ink, but with the Spirit of the living God . . . It is He who has made us competent ministers of the new covenant, a covenant not of the letter, but of the Spirit . . . (2 Cor 3:2-6).

:   And just as we accept in obediential love to be His emissaries mediating Him to others, so also we acknowledge ourselves to be in need of mediation. Because of our inherent "weakness," we see our need for a light from our fellow human beings to illuminate our darkness and overcome our inability to see God's will in moments of weakness. Authority and friends, then, become mediators of God—and a new "fraternity" is formed in a mutual response of obediential love to God's loving Providence and activity for His flock.

On the third level the Christian's intellect takes on the light of faith. In faith, there ensues an interpretation of the visible world and creatures that is unique. Grace enables us to believe that "although God dwells in unapproachable light" (1 Tm 6:16), He speaks to us by means of the whole of the universe. As St. Paul writes, "Ever since the creation of the world His invisible nature, namely His eternal power and deity, has been clearly perceived in the things that have been made" (Rm 1:20). Since we cannot conceivably encompass God and His will within the narrow limits of our reason, we seek in faith to know Him in a fuller though still limited fashion through the other levels of our being, through interaction with other human beings, and through the teaching and exhortation of the Church in particular. Not only is the intellect guided by faith, but the intellect also seeks to form itself in faith more objectively by discerning God's plan through and with others authorized by the Church, through homilies, spiritual reading, direction of superiors, etc. The will, too, is strengthened in faith enabling it to respond to God's antecedent will. The antecedent will can be defined as what God wants done prior to any decision or command of the superior. At times, a superior may make a decision that is not in accord with God's antecedent will and this decision will not appear to benefit the community or individual spiritually or psychologically. The religious must then conform to the consequent will of God in light of this erroneous but nevertheless legitimate decision of authority.[32] The religious is then called upon to make the best of a difficult situation. The logic of reason cedes to the presence of faith and trust in God's loving design, on all levels of our being, and in every supernatural movement in our life—every breath becomes a whisper of "Fiat." Grace and the Christian faith-vision of the world integrate and assume all levels into the plan of the Divine Heart—obedience becomes a response to love.

Lumen Gentium summarizes the task of the Christian as regards love:

> To seek the kingdom of God by engaging in temporal affairs and directing them according to God's will . . . There they [the laity] are called by God that, being led by the Spirit to the Gospel, they may contribute to the sanctification of the world, as from within like leaven, by fulfilling their own particular duties . . . to illuminate and order all temporal things with which they are so closely associated that these may be effected and grow according to Christ and may be to the glory of the Creator and Redeemer.[33]

B. Counsel of Obedience

The Vatican Council (*Decree on Adaptation and Renewal of Religious Life*) outlines for us the essential elements in the counsel of obedience:

> By their profession of obedience, religious offer the full surrender [dedication] of their own will as a sacrifice of themselves to God, and so are united permanently and securely to God's salvific will. After the example of Jesus Christ who came to do the Will of the Father, and 'assuming the nature of a slave' (Ph 2:7), learned obedience in the school of suffering (Heb 5:8), religious, under the motion of the Holy Spirit, subject themselves in faith to their superiors, who hold the place of God. Under their guidance they are led to serve all their brothers in Christ, just as Christ himself in obedience to the Father served his brethren and laid down his life as a ransom for many. . . . So they are closely bound to the service of the Church and strive to attain the measure of the full manhood in Christ.[34]

Now, how does religious life and the counsel of obedience fulfill the Christian response to God's loving covenant? While the counsel of obedience implies all of what is required in human and Christian obedience, it also is distinctive—in the means towards perfection which it adopts. Aquinas says: "The perfection of charity to which the counsels are directed . . . consists in man renouncing temporal things as much as possible, such as are lawful, because they occupy the mind and hinder the actual movement of the heart toward God."[35] Religious obedience is then a new duty to an old love. It is "new" in its attitude, in its even deeper conversion to Christ—its totality. How?

1. It is a public promise of a kind of obedience to which others are not obliged as Christians and simply members of the Church.[36] It is a particular means of the perfection of charity.
2. It is a calling for the Church and the world directly through total availability, with distance from every limiting tie.
3. It is a placing of one's entire existence at the disposition of God, to the point of not even knowing precisely how or for what one's gift will be used—allowing God to give form to one's whole life.[37] (Goal in faith).
4. It is a commitment to live evangelical communion in its depths, in a community and according to a community not born of flesh and blood, but which is a fruit of the Gospel and the "call" of faith. (How it is lived).[38]
5. The material object is vaster—obedience includes a gift of all one's activity, one's life, one's being, one's will, all the details of one's life, interiorly and exteriorly.[39]
6. The formal object, i.e. the motive, is an intensification and preoccupation with charity above all; one obeys out of "madlove" for Christ. A counsel is different from a virtue, although counsels are founded on virtue. It develops in the disciple a new capacity for measureless, disinterested love, sacrifice, to teach by his life, to be a model of goodness, humility, and service.[40]

In summary: Religious life incarnates an obedience of a distinctive character, an obedience that originates from the depths of the Church and is more important and total. It is one thing to live baptismal consecration in a given circumstance, and another to put this public testimony of charity at the service of the Church under the bond of a commitment taken for the whole of life. A vow made before the Church confers on obedience a sacred character. The religious takes up a sacred burden and is committed to seek out and do God's will on a daily basis in light of the constitutions and directives of superiors. There is more than just a shade of difference between Christian obedience and religious obedience.[41]

Thus, obedience is the "sacralization" of a conversion. The essence of obedience springs from an interior movement: the free act of inner conversion, the central decision of our will to let ourselves be transformed by Christ without reservation.

What does one vow in the counsel? Generally, we seek God's will exteriorly in (i) the Gospels, (ii) the Rules and Constitutions, and (iii) Ecclesial life with its tendencies, needs and directions.[42] Each of the resources for understanding God's will deserves close attention.

The Gospels are interpreted to us by pastoral letters, homilies, exhortations, by confessors, by retreat masters, by teachers, by superiors and by community. We vow to take these seriously and incorporate their wisdom into our lives through meditation, study and personal evaluation in order to determine what God asks from us.

The *Rules* and *Constitutions* are expressions of the community's discernment of God's will for us. The community as such, has the duty to announce the salvific plan of God as revealed in the Gospels for us as a whole. One's own judgment, though possibly more correct in logic or theory, at times may need to be sacrificed unless there are serious, objectively valid objections of one's conscience, and what one is asked to do is against the commandments or the greater virtue of charity. Obedience to the Rules and Constitutions also includes obedience to the superior who is recognized and authorized by the Church. A loving cooperation between superior and subject in the daily search for God's plan of salvation is essential to a healthy religious life. The heartfelt loyalty to superiors and the confidence we put in them as instruments of Christ inspire likewise the superior with willingness to entrust God's work to us in a particular way.[43] Because the superior too is a *subject*, he or she seeks to help me find the will of the Father in certain situations, and at other times to "verify and authenticate" my own interpretation of God's will. The superior/ subject relationship is a delicate one that requires a considerable amount of reflection.

The religious Constitutions prescribe detailed occasions and manners for living out God's salvific plan. Religious obedience thus enters more completely than only Christian obedience into all aspects even of our personal lives. The life style, order of the day, friends, colleagues, apostolate, habitat, prayer-forms, dress, are all largely determined by the Constitutions of our respective congregations.

We mentioned that we promise to obey the Church, the *Ecclesial Community*. This means we vow to be open and zealous about the needs of Christ in His Church as He reaches out in various ways. The Ecclesial Community offers directives, proposes changes and challenges us to deepen our commitment in serving God's people. We promise to obey the Church and its leaders as they exhort us to grow and to meet the ever changing needs of those around us.

Priestly and religious obedience are distinct from one another. Priestly obedience is more *limited*. All that is not connected to priestly ministry proper is left to the priest's discretion and personal initiative. In the field of his pastoral ministry, there are rather general norms established as a guide. The priest, however, is left considerable room for personal creativity in directing his own apostolic zeal. The obedience of a religious, however, completely envelops one's very life in all its detail.[44] If a diocesan priest wishes to be more precisely and totally consecrated, he can freely do this with the consent of his bishop and take private vows or he can join a Secular Institute. This goes beyond the promise of obedience to his bishop he made on the day of his ordination.

Given the extent to which the vow of obedience transforms our lives and demands self-sacrifice the question must be asked, "Is it worth it?" What is positive in all this? How is it useful or meaningful? What is its witness-value in this culture of independence, impulse, and self-will? The vow of obedience is a positive sign: a sign to us and to the world of four dimensions of the supernatural dynamics within the world: first, obedience is *Chris-*

tological; secondly, it is *Ecclesiological*; thirdly, it is *Eschatological*; and finally, it is *Ascetical*. Let us take these one at a time.

Christological — Although Christ was neither a religious, subject to a direct human religious superior, nor a member of the Church subject to a hierarchy,[45] His obedience, both in relation to His Father, and in relation to His apostles and disciples, was a lived submission to a simple obligation, not imposed from the outside, but a communication of life, divine life, of love.[46] Thus, Jesus' obedience is not merely a model for us to admire, but a life for us to follow. The Council Documents say: The religious not only must insert him- or herself in the mystery of Christ, but assume a model of the same obedience practiced on earth by Christ (cf. *LG* 42; *PC* 14; ET, AAS 63).

How did Christ practice obedience? a) Christ's obedience to His Father was a filial devotion of love—obedience to that love was the form and driving power and the content of His life. As religious, we too offer our lives to the Father to be transformed each day and to fulfill with a passionate love, the Father's redemptive unfolding in each movement of our being. This does not mean we are willing to offer certain behaviors to merit the love of the Father, but gratuitously to be available to a union of thoughts with the Father, and the expression of these thoughts in this world—to bring all things to Him. Just as for Jesus, this presumes that we renounce every personal project which is not in accord with His will, and strive to discern, discover, actuate His plan. Now it is true that our obedience differs from that of Jesus:

1. for us the will of the Father is not always clear, even when we search for it;[47]
2. we do not always consent as fully and radically;
3. our intensity of willing what the Father wills is different— often hampered by our own personal, human inconsistencies—effects of original sin.

Nevertheless, the Church continues to exhort us to be the light on the mountain, radiating, reflecting Christ: "to have in ourselves the same sentiments which were in Jesus Christ who stripped himself, taking the nature of a slave . . . making himself obedient unto death" (Ph 2:7-8), and "for us, from being rich, made himself poor" (2 Cor 8:9).[48] Christ's obedience was one of service, of love, transforming itself into obedience of sacrifice; a redemptive, salvific sacrifice of all He was, unto death. So is our obedience meant to be. As Christ's was a *Passive obedience*: "He handed himself over," "He never opened his mouth," "He learned to obey through suffering" as expression of his interior submission to God's will, so must ours be. As Christ's was an *Active obedience*: in relationship of Son to Father, in expressing His person, His unique intimacy with the Father (reciprocal love) by teaching, by prayer, by presence, by suffering, by involvement, by detachment, so should our obedience be.[49]

The relation of Christ to His apostles and disciples is also to be manifest, signed in religious obedience. How? For example, in the relation of superior and subject: Christ was a spiritual teacher, a listener, a healer, a challenger, a chider, a lover. So must we be—obedient to the Spirit in each other.

Ecclesiological — A second witness-value of religious obedience is to be found in its "ecclesiological" nature. Rahner writes: "Obedience is a permanent life-form, giving man a God-ward orientation. Such orientation is ecclesiological because by it the religious reveals the peculiar essence of the Church."[50] The Spirit calls religious to profess obedience not primarily and essentially for the perfection of the members and/or the community, but for an ecclesial mission (1 Cor 12:7; *LG*, 7). The vow of personal religious obedience indicates to the world that God wants the sanctification of His people in a Christian assembly, in a hierarchic, ordered Church-community of mutual availability. The religious community is a sign of the Church community and of the Covenant of which the Church is the concrete realization. It is an indication to the faithful of how obedience in the Church is evangelically based—as a practice of loving submission toward authority lived in the people of God, of loving active cooperation in the redemptive plan under the guidance and mediation of the Spirit. Religious obedience is living, as the Church does, the fullness of the mystery of death and resurrection. It reminds the people of God of our call, as the Church's, to service, to availability, to suffering as a participation in the oblation of Christ. Religious obedience indicates to them the loving communication of God concretized in mutual, trusting dialogue, and final surrender to a higher destiny which we see now only in a "veiled" manner. This obedience is a sign of the Church's exclusive dedication of its energies to the concerns of the Lord and what is pleasing to Him.

Thus it is vital to remember that not only are we witnesses to Christ's universal love and availability in love to redeem His sons and daughters, but by our vow of religious obedience we witness the Church's universal concerns and love. Therefore, as one author puts it clearly:

> Consecrated obedience is not a reality which concerns only the interior of our institute. It is an *ecclesial* fact above all because it is 'a divine gift which the Church has received from Our Lord' (*LG* 43). The Church gathers and offers it up in union with the oblation of the Eucharistic sacrifice (*LG* 45): 'This is my body given up for you.' Thus there is expressed in the Liturgy the fecundity of consecrated obedience (the apostolic dimension of the contemplative).[51]

Therefore, religious obedience is a consecration of the person to the good of the *whole* Church—to strengthen in souls the reign of Christ and to spread it to every part of the earth. For proper discernment of God's will, both the needs of the universal and the local Church must be considered. A smaller community must make its decisions in the context of the greater ecclesial communion, not only listening to the life of the Church and its needs, but also listening to those pastors who have received their ministry in apostolic succession.[52] Therefore obedience is a full consecration to the mission of the Church universal in that it manifests the Church in that environment discerned as the one most appropriate for the person, according to the charisms and gifts distributed by the Spirit (*LG* 46; *PC* 1-2). All personal gifts are given for the purpose of building up the Church and its functioning as the Body of Christ (Ep 2:12; 1 Cor 13).

In a word, then, the vow of obedience renders us signs of the Church; available to serve the universal loving will of God, and eager to discern for self and others wherein lies that will here and now, and to assist one toward its fulfillment.[53]

Eschatological — Sign of Eternity. To put it briefly, the vow of obedience is a witness of eternity—a manifestation of the power of other-worldly grace and an acceptance of surrender by faith alone. In spite of one's impatience, religious obedience indicates that there can be, will be, and is, a mystical union of wills between the Father and the Son, between the Father, the Son, and ourselves—a completion of the Covenant: I will be your God, you will be my people, even in eternity. Obedience is a reminder that the power of love is infinite, and surrender to that love results in union of wills. Obedience is a sign that the Kingdom of God is present because we declare ourselves totally available to the will of the other who is God and who calls us to eternal union. Thus, under the vow of obedience, that which could be a failure, a deviation of this or that particular part of being or existence, becomes integrated in a superior eternal order and plan—where there can be no failures, but simply redemptive meaning in the global plan of a loving Master.

Therefore, from these three kinds of witness given by the vow of obedience: witness of Christ, of the Church, of Eternal Life— we perceive the positive richness of the vow of obedience. Obedience is not principally a submission for its own sake. It is an availability, an offer of accessibility to the completion of the Divine Alliance, the Covenant of Love for oneself and for the people of God. "If you follow me, then I will be your God, and you will be my people." Obedience is a realization of the highest level and most total hierarchic ordering of the natural levels in us, in response to the supernatural, which facilitates an expression of Faith so radical, so clear, it can shine on the mountain top. While the vow of obedience is an annulling, a "no" to all that is self-centered, individualistic, egocentric, to all that is limiting in our plans and being, it opens us up to a multiplicity of relations in the community of the people of God; to motives more pure, universal and infinite—as pure Divine Love; to service which is more effective and eternal; to a will which is stronger and more universally and Divinely oriented; to an intellect which is freed to reach beyond reason into faith. In a word, this consecration of religious obedience is the invasion of love, given at the moment of baptismal consecration with the gift of the Spirit (Rm 5:5), which goes on developing to such a point that it takes possession of us in all our dimensions and brings us beyond them into Him more purely.

Yet, on the other hand, the vow of obedience, by its very nature also implies a renunciation of certain levels, certain means, only to arrive at a fuller reality. One psychiatrist puts it this way: "It is by repeatedly consenting to the satisfaction of certain needs and refusing to satisfy others, that human dynamism develops throughout the greater part of man's life in certain special directions."[54] The same is applicable to supernatural growth as integrated with human growth. Let's study this renunciation— what surrenders are asked of us in this vow and to what end?

Ascetical — The dimension of renunciation: "If a man wishes to come after me, he must deny his very self, take up his cross and begin to follow in my footsteps" (Mt 16:24-26).

Christian asceticism, although actually first a "yes" to the God of the supernatural life, is also a "yes" to that manner of grace working in the fate of Jesus, leading him to the Cross and death. It is a filling up of what is wanting in the passion of Christ, insofar as it is an act of faith in that love-pact which was finally achieved on the Cross, for the reconciliation of the world with God.[55] Choice of one value above others always includes renunciation of others. It necessitates the letting go of some potential wishes or decisions for other ones to be actualized.[56] So it is with obedience. The personal realization of the higher values of the supernatural by comparison with the merely human good, even moral good, can ultimately be achieved only by the free sacrifice of worldly goods, so that through the darkness, the death-trend, the pain, the finiteness and the vanity of our own will, we learn to lay ourselves open to God, in faith and love—open to His "incomprehensible decree."[57]

Religious obedience is a real participation in the Cross of Christ, so that through it one can enter into His glory. The obedient religious, however, is a "lover"—and as for any lover, the sacrifice of self-surrender is a paradox: while it is actually deeply painful at times, it is more profoundly a delight, delight in the union and similarity with Christ. But, what is involved in this self-surrender in the vow of obedience, what does one renounce? Some of the world's most treasured keepsakes: the right to erect one's own little world in a more or less undisturbed, autonomous way; the right to power, to self-disposal which is rewarded in this life; the right to desire, decide, to choose according to rational and/or created values which are good and satisfying and fulfilling. We agree to let our Lover make demands on us even when we do not desire to be constrained. Out of love we act even when we do not wish to and accept suffering even when we would rather avoid it. In obedience we understand that our Lover will require at times that we be alone when we would rather be with someone and be with someone when we would rather be alone. We ask Him to call us to Himself and His design when we tend to be lost in ourselves, in our own small plans. This renunciation, made as a consecration to *the* Beloved, transforms and fulfills us: "Thus, religious obedience, far from diminishing the dignity of the human person, helps it to grow to its full development having expanded us to the liberty of the Sons of God."[58] The gift of trust we made to God becomes the gift of love He makes to us—He values us and entrusts us again with His design, transforming us ever closer to His will, to His Heart.

Through this dynamic process of asceticism, this renunciation by the counsel of obedience, a number of virtues are simultaneously called for and lived. What are these virtues?

1) *Faith*[59] — Religious obedience is a commitment of oneself to listen to the Gospel, to Christ in His unfathomable daily mystery. It is essentially an act of belief in the invisible God, from whom every order ensues, and because of Him, it is also an act of trust in whoever is the instrument of which God makes use to transmit this order. The demands of faith oftentimes cannot be made reasonable to an observer: the call of God to die to one's pride, to one's own plans for self, is never reasonable by any standards except faith. Bonhoeffer says (reflecting Kierkegaard): "When God calls man, He bids him come and die." Only faith can make sense of this for one who loves life.

2) *Hope* — Obedience is an offering of faith in a focusing on God alone, while yet bearing the trials of life with fortitude, allowing hope to energize life here. Hope is the expectation that God will one day be the *all*, the absolute all of my weakened will and vacillating yes of surrender. Hope is the offspring of our faith and parent of true love—of total *adsum* (presence).

3) *Love*[60] — Religious obedience is a response to love in two ways: first of all, we are asked to read the will of God in daily events with the eyes of love, to see that if the Father requests such in our regard it is because He loves us passionately, even if this will is crucifying. Love recognizes love in obedience. Secondly, when we become so disinterested regarding our own will, and surrender ourselves so fully to Him and to His people, love becomes both pure and purifying. Even if everything is lawful, the religious, by obedience, acknowledges that not everything is harmless. Although lawful, everything may not be for the good of others (1 Cor 14:1-19). This is love; this is obedience to truth and God's delicate working in each human soul. Thus, renouncing even the *lawful*, in seeking in no way our own advantage, but that of others, we live a love that is a Divine reflection of His own immolation. Renunciation is the deepest symbol of love; love then becomes an eschatological virtue, a sign of infinite fullness of love in Him only in eternity. Love has no norms by which it can be measured; obedience is then, not response to a set of norms, but to an Infinite Love.

> When a lesser love refuses to become the greater, (even eternal)
>   it is no love at all.
> When we refuse to surrender our wills to His,
>   there is no love.

4) *Mercy*[61] — In leaving our lives in His hands in obedience, we offer our lives to carry His compassion to the poor, the blind, those suffering from social injustice, those deprived of their freedom, or living with broken hearts, to sinners, to those needing mercy though they do not realize it.[62] We offer ourselves as messengers of mercy in crises; and the crises which enter human

life are not confined to the surface, but touch the depth of the human soul. It is where a person's richest perfections are that the most serious losses can be sustained, and mercy, like the generosity of God, should extend to these depths.[63] We offer ourselves as liaisons between the Father and humanity, as Christ. Through merciful love we wish to be such a bridge. At the same time we manifest a faith in His loving mercy in our own lives, trusting that He will be merciful in His commands and in His promises, in His bending down to us in loving fidelity. Religious obedience is a sign of St. Paul's words: "We carry this treasure in vessels of clay to show that the abundance of the power is God's and not ours" (2 Cor 4:7). We are evidence of His living mercy: there is mercy among people through us and our obedience, because there is mercy in God, because there is God's love.

5) *Humility-Docility*[64] — Obedience is an expression of an interior truth, an ordering of reality as regards Creator and creature. We are His creature, and, with Christ, we cry: "The Father is greater than I" (Jn 14:28). This is humble surrender to His rightful place in our life. It is an admission of the limitation of our own human condition, and of our need to be saved. We cannot be saved without openness to mediation; this is obedience. Finally, the condition of our communion with the Lord, with our Creator, is that humility, that readiness to serve others whom the Lord provides for us, to "wash their feet." We are ready to empty ourselves daily as He did, in humility, in humble obedience.

6) *Justice*[65] — Religious obedience is an acknowledgment and respect of the people of God as persons, as members of a corporate mystical body also in need of redemption. It is a sign that in our wounded equality we are willing to reach out in giving what we so mercifully received—that all may be one. We are willing in religious obedience, in community, to give each person what is necessary to play his or her part in the external order of the universe, directed to God, and in this, in the order of His Plan, to achieve, likewise as for us, union with God.

7) *Patience*[66] — Now if we have sincerely and totally abandoned our wills to the Father, a "waiting" will be asked of us. We will often walk in darkness, waiting for the realization of His

plans in our life; we will wait for the accomplishment of His life, His Kingdom, in slow paces in our own day by day existence, and in those of our brothers and sisters. Dryness, darkness, anxiety, confusion, uncertainty will be constant companions to us because of the "risk" we have taken in faith. Patient hope is the only remedy. If impatience stems from a feeling of unrestrained pride, patience, in obediential surrender, is the only remedy to such a self-indulgence and lack of acceptance of truth. Patience means preservation of the right order in our lives. It means God is sovereign and His will is our all. Patience helps us to acknowledge others who have goals as sincere as ours, and to recognize that they also are burdened like ourselves in their struggle to rise and live in His faithful, guiding love. We need patience with ourselves and God and others in daily obedience: only the patient person who lives by Christ can persevere unto the end and "possess his soul" in fullness of obedience (Lk 21:19).

IV. CHARACTERISTICS OF MATURE RELIGIOUS OBEDIENCE

What do the Church documents and the Gospels call us to concretely in this vow of obedience? What attitudes and capacities must we develop if we are to be given profoundly and holily (Whole-ily) to His will only? Let us list and discuss a few of the characteristics which we should find in ourselves, in our own obedience in community.

A. Co-responsibility[67]

Religious cannot renounce their use of autonomous responsibility and freedom totally to the Superior because the Superior has given permission or "blesses" some action.

Obedience cannot be made to bear the *whole* burden of a person's spiritual life and way of life, of decisions and guidance.[68]

This would be infantilism. In fact, I may have to do things at times which are not to the "liking" of the Superior, but which are still *obedient*.

Co-responsibility means that each member should actively and responsibly participate in the discerning process, sustained by the charisms which the Holy Spirit "dispenses among all the faithful of every order" (*LG* 12). Co-responsibility (not merely for discerning, but for self-control) is founded on faith, and faith is concretized by subsidiarity and decentralization—a sharing of the responsibility with all the chosen of God who together "seek to discern in the events, in the requests, and in the aspirations of each, what are the true signs of the presence and design of God, and live them out faithfully" (*GS* 46). Co-responsible members constantly seek to choose those circumstances and situations which will help them and others to contemplate God more fully. "The personal conscience must have a presence of responsible evaluation on what is commanded and which must be followed according to obedience" (St. Thomas, *De Veritate*, q. 17, a.5). This, of course, means that we must be persons of the Kingdom of God.

B. Persons of the Kingdom of God

Our only aim should be to perceive and live the Divine thoughts, to be sensible to the interior revealed word, having the same "tastes" as Jesus (Ph 2:5). This means to seek for a wisdom not of this world, "the wisdom of this world is useless before God" (1 Cor 2:14). We seek rather to transcend every utilitarian, earthly goal and allow ourselves to be guided by faith. A constant discerning heart is necessary.

C. A Constancy and Stability in Discerning Objectively

The conscience of a religious always seeks to examine with the Superior, with members of the group and the Constitutions of the

Institute, with the Church, with one's own inner disposition, with one's psycho-social direction, what decision more realistically conforms to the will of the Father for the individual. This means a religious should be capable of distinguishing between unrealistic idealization and expectations and down-to-earth possibilities of witness in response to the obediential call.[69] A global discernment, then, means one cannot limit oneself always and enclose oneself in the Institutional rule always, for at times, what is "lawful" may not even be prudent, and vice versa. A discerning religious must be attentive to the will of God beyond the rule also, through the needs of the ecclesial community, the desires and constructive analyses and suggestions of others, the kind of work in which they are involved. This discernment, of course, requires a constant, reflective attitude—reflection on my own consciousness and its limits, on the courses of action readily available, and the uncertainties and risks they involve. In other words, we need to ask questions (1) about ourselves; (2) about the object itself, i.e. what is the proposed course of action; (3) about consequences of the action; (4) about motives for the action; and (5) about its consistency with Gospel values. We should also maintain a facility to reflect even on these reflections—after the decision has been made, discerning honestly the consequences of it. Therefore, discernment is necessary in order not to "obstruct the action of the Holy Spirit. Do not depreciate the messages of God: examine all things and keep that which is good" (1 Th 5:19-21). Now, if discernment is necessary, one must have a capacity to listen.

D. A Capacity to Listen

No authority or subject is able to interpret with objectivity and a relative confidence the spiritual good of self or another if they are not able, first of all, to allow the possibility of opening their hearts to each other with a friendly, filial spirit (LG 20, 24, 27, 28). Lumen Gentium calls us to this, and authors constantly reiterate the need for this basic capacity: "When treating of singular members, the norm seems to be not to judge anyone without first hearing him."[70] If one is able to listen, then there is the possibility of an honest dialogue.

E. Openness to Dialogue [71]

Dialogue is a preliminary step to decision. Any decision to be made should be made in a spirit of mutual openness and trust. Each person, superior and subject, should try to enter into the mind of the other, always ready to extend, renew or change their own point of view. Dialogue should be sincere, open, without rigidity and prejudice; "there should be no *a priori* condemnation, nor offensive and habitual polemics." Cardinal Garrone, reviewing *Ecclesiam Suam* and the section on the art of spiritual communication (nn. 51, 52), presents four characteristics of mature dialogue:

1. clarity—through exercise of the higher faculties of the person;
2. affability—peaceful, patient, generous, not proud, or pungent, or offensive;
3. confidence—trust in the value of the word each speaks as well as the disposition of each party;
4. prudence—know the sensibilities of the other, keep in mind the moral and psychological dispositions of each, and present discussions in an opportune way.

Now, truth and sincerity, lack of prejudice in dialogue, can be brought about if they are built on a deep interiorized *respect* for individuals and trust in them. We need to value the individual.

F. Valuing the Individual [72]

Both superiors and subjects must be very much in touch with their own poverty, that is, the awareness that alone as individuals we may not be able to see fully our own total good nor the common good. Vatican II calls for collaboration of many individuals so that the common good may be richer and more complete. This means that we need to value each other, to accept and *wish* others different from ourselves so that we may be mutually enriched, open to deeper solutions, different visions and means all within the framework of the Gospels, the Church, the Institute. What a disaster it would be if our body was all hands, society was all female or all male, bosses or clerks, bus drivers or mayors! To wish someone else to think exactly as we do, to do as we do, to feel as we do, is to deny and deprive them of the differential quality of the charisms and intentions of the Holy Spirit working in them: this is a wish to deny individuality, the basis of real freedom and real obedience. Thus, there must be a mutual trust that we are all here to "do His will"—as the Spirit ordains in His own valuing and call of the person, in all his uniqueness. Now, if there is a genuine valuing of the individual person, there can be greater respect and valuing of the common good and a smooth complementarity.

G. Complementarity: Valuing the Common Good[73]

When individuals find joy in each other's gifts of the Spirit and enrichment in them, there will ensue a complementarity which fosters mutual help and favors an active relationship of *communion*. Each member, in faith and joy, respecting and valuing the competences of each one at his level, is eager for communion with the others, as open and poor (as limited, often) as themselves, to reconfirm from time to time, to re-discern from time to time their charisms and ministry, to orient themselves more fully, in fidelity to the Spirit, to the greater good of the Church, of the Institute. Thus, together we come to ask, not what does the community want, but what does the community believe God wants of it. Individuality, and the value of the individual or group, are then posited in their proper perspective—instruments in God's loving design, as He has planned in our being, for redeeming, for calling to conversion.

The variety of gifts has raised up a variety of religious communities of consecrated life (*PC* 1); but, in each of them, by the new distribution of charisms or ministries, which the Holy Spirit foresees (provides) regarding each member (*LG* 12), there is verified a complementary variety of competence, and therefore of roles. All, however, is clearly willed and ordained by the Spirit to form an organic whole with articulated responsibilities, which, by active cooperation, build up in charity the entire body (Ep 4:7-16).

Thus, love of the charisms of the Spirit in each member raises one's self-esteem, and assists individuals to perform their apostolic activity with deeper joy, not in their own name but in the name of the loving, obedient community, which sends them; this is working towards the common good, the common goals of the Institute. The work of *one* becomes the work of *all*, and God is twice glorified. The complementarity for the common good presupposes in each person a solid, internalized Gospel value system.

H. Internalization of Gospel Values

A religious will obey willingly if he or she has, through trial and effort, and struggle, in joy and in sorrow, constantly formed his will in acts of selflessness in faith. We must not merely believe in the values of Christ, but we must bring our own personal ideals into a consistent relation to these values of Christ, the Church, the community. We can ask ourselves if the Gospel values are internalized in us, with the following questions:

1. Am I ready to respond without being recognized or rewarded by others?
2. Am I willing to die to those parts of me that are not in keeping with the Infinite love-pact?
3. Will I give *all* of myself, consumed for the salvation of souls, forgetful of myself?

If one can answer yes, it is probable that the value of obedience has deep roots, is internalized *for itself*; that means that one has the natural "ground" consistent and fertile for the workings of the call to self-surrender. Therefore, to support values, we need a psychologically mature personality.

I. A Psychologically Mature Personality[74]

If we are healthy in our own self-esteem, knowledgeable about ourselves, we will be able realistically to value with a deep sense of awe and gratitude our real personal potentialities and gifts. At the same time, we will be keenly aware of our own personal limits, acknowledging the need for the charisms of others. A mature personality can be authentic in the vow of obedience because such persons are masters of their own spontaneous reactions. Such people use their intellect and reason and can go beyond their own personal interests, taking a more objective view, unencumbered by distressing emotional judgments, being free and uninfluenced by prejudices or personal preferences in making choices. The mature person seeks to give constructively to the community and to be with others in a warm personal way. At the same time mature people do not attempt to escape the necessary solitude that accompanies the "yes" of their Gethsemanes. In a word, research (Rulla, et al.) clearly indicates that decisions and discernment will be as objective as the person is profoundly integrated, on all levels.

Thus, a mature, effective living out of the vow of obedience, springing from an interiority that is hierarchically ordered will manifest itself in vitality and all the fruits of the Spirit (Mt 7:16), such as love, joy, peace, patience, kindness, goodness, fidelity, gentleness, and self-control. No laws can force such fruits (Gal 5:22-23). The law of love prevails in a tried but faithful ADSUM in an integrated personality.

A psychologically mature personality is the result of a balance in the person of his own needs (both conscious and unconscious) and his values, as well as of his attitudes. The consistency between one's conscious ideals of obedience and his actual self living out the obedience, (conscious and unconscious) or interpreting the obedience more or less objectively, will lead to greater capacity for self transcendence as well as satisfaction in his vowed, existential obedience. Vice versa, if one is inconsistent deep within—i.e. when there is inconsistency between one's values and needs and attitudes, inconsistency between what one thinks he is and with what he wants to be, and with what he *really* is and desires and seeks inside his inner depths of the psyche, then abuses or distortions of obedience will more easily occur in one's life.

The following schema, adapted from L.M. Rulla's "Vicious Circle" of Entering Religious Vocationers or of Drop Outs (1981), by Sr. Anna Bissi, can also be applied concretely thus:

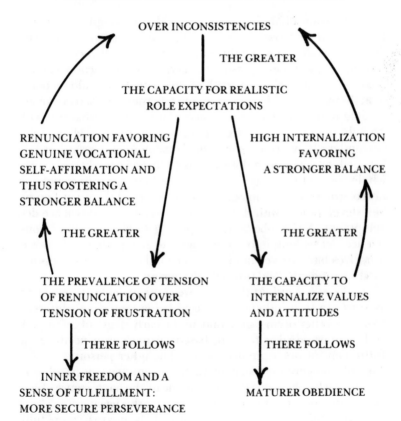

THE GREATER THE PREVALENCE OF CONSISTENCIES

OVER INCONSISTENCIES

THE GREATER

THE CAPACITY FOR REALISTIC
ROLE EXPECTATIONS

RENUNCIATION FAVORING
GENUINE VOCATIONAL
SELF-AFFIRMATION AND
THUS FOSTERING A
STRONGER BALANCE

HIGH INTERNALIZATION
FAVORING
A STRONGER BALANCE

THE GREATER

THE GREATER

THE PREVALENCE OF TENSION
OF RENUNCIATION OVER
TENSION OF FRUSTRATION

THE CAPACITY TO
INTERNALIZE VALUES
AND ATTITUDES

THERE FOLLOWS

THERE FOLLOWS

INNER FREEDOM AND A
SENSE OF FULFILLMENT:
MORE SECURE PERSEVERANCE

MATURER OBEDIENCE

V. INTERFACE BETWEEN THE HUMAN AND THEOLOGICAL ELEMENTS IN MATURE RELIGIOUS OBEDIENCE

A. Differentiation, Unity, Integration of Person as a Presupposition

Levels of Ego Development (Loevinger)[75]

If the counsel of obedience means that we re-gift Christ and His Church with our entire self, then we must *be* a self first in order to be able to make this gift. If mature obedience means a capacity of awareness, personal discernment, interaction with an openness to others, to the truth of the Gospels, to stand on one's feet, there must be a basic underlying integrated human personality able to do this. How do we arrive at maturity; what levels of growth underlie our differing responses to the call to self-surrender? Why are we sometimes unable to go forward or call forward, or dialogue and discern as easily as we might wish? The whole issue of development comes up here. Jane Loevinger, a noted American psychologist, has a researched theory of Ego or Self development with differing stages related to conscience development. Since obedience implies a "right objective" conscience, let us look into these stages, to see, perhaps where we ourselves have arrived, and to understand our own readiness for total surrender to God through our person.

a. Presocial Level. At this level, we come to delineate ourselves as separate from others: a sense of being "someone" different from the other occurs, generally in the early stages of infancy. A rudimentary ideal is formed, based on one's own needs, even fulfillment of one's physical needs. The other person is merely "useful," no genuine social interaction or mutuality is possible. A religious who obeys another because he or she has no sense of self and cannot do without the other, is here at this level.

b. Impulsive Level. At this level, the child begins to be more fully filled with and preoccupied with his own wishes and impulses which serve to affirm and consolidate the sense of self. There are no inner controls yet, and the environment functions to teach impulse control by reward and punishment. The child avoids doing harm by turning his aggression against himself, and feeling ashamed and guilty, so as to desist from anything contrary to the "rules" given. So, for example, if a religious sister obeys simply because she would feel ashamed or guilty if she did *not* obey, or only because "Sister said so" and "We'd better obey, or else," she is at this level. If she seeks always to get what *she* wants at all costs and the heck with everyone else, she is here at this level.

c. Self-Protective Level. At this level the child is preoccupied with harm-avoidance; that is, seeking to avoid both inner and outer dangers. The child gains control over impulses which may seem dangerous, and learns to postpone gratification when it is useful or expedient to do so. Very often there is a swaying from a general complete submission to bursts of dominative display which subside quickly. There is both vulnerability present and a budding sense of security in the ongoing success at mastering the environment and the self (for one's own self-protection).

A religious who is at this level may obey erratically: generally haltingly submissive and agreeable, but with a tell-tale outburst of passive resistance or domination which quickly subsides. Such a religious is seeking to master both sides of his or her personality: to feel secure in accepting control by others without losing the sense of self, and to feel secure in mastering others, dominating others.

d. Conformist Level. At this level the problem of self-protection and autonomy is resolved. How? By identification with authority. One identifies completely with the controlling powers, and thus in some way subconsciously one feels a share in their domination. This level is reached by most but not by all children. Parental precepts and standards are accepted because they are sources of vicarious power and domination, without the threatening risks. A religious at this level would identify completely with the standards, visions, means and suggestions of the superior or institution, because "they know more" and "they have more experience," or because "everyone is going, or everyone is doing it, and we have to be there." There is conformity to rules regardless of means or consequences. "I wear a pair of shoes until I am crippled because the rule says . . ."

e. Conscientious Level. At this level the youngster begins to internalize rules; i.e. learning to evaluate himself, selecting rules to be followed, discerning their value, and administering rules and sanctions to himself. Self-ideals are extended to a wider social unit than one's own family, and one acts on an inner obligation for one's own welfare and that of others. There is, then, enjoyment of mutual love and respect. A religious at this level obeys because there is *value* and meaning in the request for reasons relevant not merely to oneself, but to others; e.g. a sister turns off the TV at the superior's request because she knows she has something good to offer and receive from others.

f. Autonomous-Integrated Level. At this level the young adult learns or comes to be able to tolerate moral ambiguity without disintegration or an inner sense of gnawing guilt and moral condemnation. Such people are capable of a disinterested balancing of their success and failures and can take responsibility for both without defensive maneuvers, planning in a realistic way for achieving their disinterested objective ideals, tolerating individual differences while going ahead. A religious sister who can obey with a clear sense of her limitedness and failures, and who can, nevertheless, find and create a constructive plan for realizing her union with Christ, within the framework of others, of the suggestions and orders of superiors, is functioning from this level. She is not threatened by individual differences, as already remarked; she can tolerate ambiguities and make distinctions between essentials and what is peripheral. She is open, sensitive, and flexible, but clear and stable in following her means to *His* goal in her life.

One can clearly see, therefore, how these "human" levels of development leave shadows in our life of faith and religious obedience—how they can color our ideal of total self-surrender. Interestingly, Jane Loevinger has shown that there are in actuality only a small number of people who have reached the last level.

How does this fit in with the levels of moral development which are contemporaneously existing in us? Laurence Kohlberg has identified six stages in our moral development.[76]

Levels of Moral Development (Kohlberg)

a. Pre-Conventional Level:

Stage 1: Punishment and Obedience Orientation

Here an action is seen as good or bad depending on the physical consequences of it. So the goal is to avoid punishment, and there is unquestioning deference to power. For example: I obey so I can have my vacation, to avoid getting called in.

Stage 2: The Instrumental-Relativist Orientation

Here right action is that which satisfies one's needs; it is the "you scratch my back, and I'll scratch yours" stage. I obey because if I listen to you, you will listen to me. These first two stages are called *pre-conventional*, as the individual's social perspective is of not belonging to the group. At these stages, too, consequences are immediate and obvious.

b. Conventional Level:

Stage 3: Interpersonal Concordance: Good Boy, Nice Girl Orientation

Here good behavior is what pleases or helps others, or is approved by them. By "being nice" one earns approval and thinks of oneself as acting obediently, rightly. The objective rule counts little as such.

Stage 4: Law and Order Orientation

Right behavior consists in doing one's duty, respecting authority and the social order for its own sake. Authority, fixed rules, maintenance of social order, are important for their own sake. I obey for the good of order in the house; to help the community function smoothly; I must do it. Stages three and four make up the conventional level, where the social perspective is that of the member of the group or of society; here the expectations of others are regarded as valuable in their own right.

c. Post-Conventional Level:

Stage 5: Social Contract-Legalistic Orientation

Here there is an emphasis on the legal point of view, but with the possibility of changing the law through rational consideration of its social utility (stage 4 would be too rigid for that). Free agreement and contract are the binding elements of obligation at this stage. I obey because I said I would, it fits my rights and is accepted by all.

Stage 6: Universal Ethical Principle Orientation

Here the right and the good are defined by the decision of conscience in accord with self chosen ethical principles appealing to logical comprehensiveness, universality, and consistency. I obey because it is just. I respect the rights and dignity of all as individual persons. Very few people arrive at this stage of moral reasoning, but along with the work of Loevinger, Kohlberg's findings show a general movement of development: from exterior control of our being, decisions and actions, to a more personal control, though still influenced by punishment or reward, by approval or disapproval; to more objective control of our actions because of and according to disinterested, universal principles worthy of our obedience in themselves. If conscience is mature there may be a sense of accountability for actions, feelings, obligations, in themselves; a capacity for self-critique and clearly defined standards and ideals. How few have reached this sort of human integration! Both Loevinger and Kohlberg have found that there is no strict correspondence between chronological age and psychological growth and development.

While we are including the theories of Loevinger, and to a lesser extent that of Kohlberg here, as relatable in some way to the processes presupposed or useful for a mature obedience in general, some specifications and criticisms should be included as regards these theorists.

a. Both Loevinger's and Kohlberg's theories tend to take the view that growth or development occurs in a coherent, progressive way, touching different aspects of the personality in a more-or-less unified manner. Loevinger, e.g. follows a hierarchic model of development: each stage builds on the former completed stage; nothing is left behind. In a strict sense this may be an incompatible and foreign personality model for consideration on religious obedience, with the assumption of subconscious inconsistencies, the model adopted here. Loevinger, for example (1976), expresses the view that ego development occurs by a series of transformations which touch at least many if not all the aspects of the personality in a coherent way (B. Kiely, S.J. summarizes precisely this aspect on pp. 109-112 of *Psychology and Moral Theology*).

Now it is important to keep in mind, however, that if one aspect of ego development is mature, this does not necessarily mean that the *whole person* is mature. For example: one may proclaim values of obedience, but because of emotional factors tied to underlying subconscious inconsistencies, one may be unable to live them out. Kohlberg, too, can be critiqued here, because it has been found that despite high levels of moral reasoning, people have been found to be psychopathic at times in their behavior.

This is to say, then, that although one may have "developed" in their "ego" or in their cognitive moral reasoning capacities, they will not *necessarily* then follow through on living Gospel values radically. Thus, there is no one-to-one direct relationship between ego development, moral reasoning, and living out "automatically" the vow of obedience. This *does* wish to suggest, however, vice versa: that a person who has internalized the virtue and vow of obedience, most likely does have a sufficient capacity for moral reasoning and decision making as well as a sufficiently integrated and developed ego to sustain and carry out the burdens, often, of a mature choice in obedience.

b. Other critiques to keep in mind: some authors have called Kohlberg "biased against religion." While this may be an exaggeration, it should nevertheless be kept in mind that Kohlberg does deal with only an "autonomous human value," that of justice.

Insofar as his system is concerned, it is to be remembered that Kohlberg is concerned *only* with justice. For him justice is the only "virtue" (1981), and moral reasoning in Kohlberg's method is purely cognitive in its terms. He is dealing with only a small part of the whole personality. If Kohlberg's standard of measure is taken as a reflection of all of the personality or all values, then confusion is bound to result. Religious obedience strictly speaking lies outside the domain of Kohlberg's research (see Kiely, p. 64, par. 2 and 3). Kohlberg's research is thus subordinate even to Loevinger's. However, if current research in progress (Rulla, Imoda, Ridick) tends to prove that the process of internalization is related to the presence of consistencies or inconsistencies which are subconscious in one's dynamics, and includes the integration of objective Gospel values, *as well as* mature human values (natural values), then Kohlberg's "human" aspect of a very partial area of moral development may be useful insofar as a partial perspective of human, rational development is concerned. It should, then, be considered as *among those elements* to be considered in an internalized value system.[77]

If we take into account the *many* aspects of development, cognitive, emotional, etc., is it any wonder, then, that we have difficulty on occasion in communication, in discernment, in accepting the invitations or prescriptions of our religious superiors? Psychological inconsistencies (the interior tension or *war*, an effect of original sin) tend to pull us in differing directions: toward proclaimed values of our own as well as institutional and Gospel values, on the one hand; and toward gratification of personal needs, often fixated at some developmental level, on the other hand.[78]

VI. USES AND ABUSES OF OBEDIENCE

So far we have presented the ideals of mature obedience in the religious life; then we discussed some factors in our own human development as persons or as moral beings (judging ethically) which in some real sense color our availability to living out this religious obedience in its fullness. Now, limited as we are by these differing developmental levels, let us see how these limitations surface and exhibit themselves in some distortions or abuses regarding the vow of obedience, our response to the call to do His will.

A. First Level

1. Comfort (physical, e.g. to avoid fatigue, anxiety, etc.)

On the first level, if the physiological level of satisfaction has become a goal in our lives rather than a means, we may often choose or discern what we can and should do, or are told to do by our superiors, according to the goal of achieving comfort, avoiding fatigue or anxiety or incompleteness of any sort. "Naturalism" becomes our religion and we refuse to accept anything that makes demands upon us even on a physical level. On the other hand, if our mid-life has been marked by penance, by the surrender of our whole self including the physical, to the direction of God, we come to accept and endure the increasing detachment which aging entails. "We rely upon the grace of the divine life direction as it manifests itself from day to day. It is more an attitude of waiting than a bracing ourselves to execute *sternly* divine directions."[79] We come during later stages of life, in advancing age, to continue to hand over to the Lord our entire lives including our bodies. The more we grow in the disposition that we want God to do with us as He wishes, then the more we are really ready in obedience for the disappointments and debilitations which the later years have in store for us. Obedience implies readiness for pain, fatigue, incompleteness, even on a physical level. Escapism for comfort's sake is an avoidance of obedience.

2. Excessive drive

There are those of us religious, on the other hand, who may be on the opposite end of the see-saw, i.e. those who can never sit down, are always on the go, needing to do, to talk, to act. This excess (though generally rarer in this day and age) is an abuse of obedience too, since it very likely leaves little time or opportunity to place oneself before the Lord and listen—listen to Him directly, and also to others. One's own plans and drives become the goal of existence.

B. Second Level

1. Compliance[80]

Compliance is the acceptance of an order or exhortation primarily for the motive of avoiding punishment or receiving reward. On this level, one acts—or rather, one "reacts" to an order or request on account of the material benefit which can accrue, e.g. I can be elected superior next year; or they will put me on a committee; or they will allow me to make final vows; or the next time I see them, they'll have nothing to "call me down for," or criticize me for. Thus, the obedience stems from an underlying attempt to be the "nice girl or good boy," so as to keep things peaceful and comfortable for oneself. Fransen says: "One point should be clear: God wants our *hearts*, not conformism; not even the most pious [conformism] can satisfy God's demands. Our hearts have been given to us in order that we may return them."[81] We are free and filially submitted to a Divine Father insofar as we are living out of conviction, from love and not from fear.

These compliant "obeyers" are those who hesitate to speak their minds on anything, even being unwilling to discuss behavior which is obviously against the will of God. It is true that a distinction should be made between criticism and discernment; but while these people do engage in criticism (close-minded, self-righteous judgment of others, according to exterior standards), they are not mature enough to dialogue or discern with another what seems to be problematic with regard to obedience. Dialogue as an expression of mature obedience presents a challenge, especially to one who is alive, genuine, and rich in a spirit of faith. But if we sink into mediocrity and compliance and cut ourselves off from real life and begin to capitulate and compromise, and in this "humanly defective state" continue on in religious life, then we are living a lesser calling while being asked by the Master to follow Him in something greater. If we come to the point of only "enduring" religious life, mitigating our responsibilities and involvements and sinking into a compliant, mediocre existence, then we have missed the meaning and purpose of obedience.

2. Non-Internalizing Identification[82]

Non-internalizing identification is the process whereby we obey a rule or command for the social benefits that will accrue to us; e.g., obeying as a member of a group so as to gratify certain needs of ours such as dependency, or exhibition, or achievement. That is, we obey not for the value of the principle involved in the request itself, but because we are a "part of the group." How often this occurs! We go to the meeting, or we meet for prayer, or we obey, because Sister or Father So-and-so does—to keep their friendship and support them. Now, friendship is no obstacle to obedience unless it ceases to be genuine friendship and becomes dependency or "two person egotism," as one author puts it.[83] Generally this weakness or limitation of non-internalizing identification comes from a fixation on a developmental level of the past where relations with others were functional: one obeyed because one was thereby "accepted." "The child or adolescent who felt important because he was useful to someone, because he knew how to do many things, or because he felt threatened in his existence if he did not render the service requested, will continue as an adult to feel 'someone' only if he can do something for others (like others) or channel his energies into a continuous activity."[84] Take away the gifts, the cards, the service, this so-called "obedience," and the relationship ends or one's identity collapses. "The General Superior did not come to visit me or call"; "The Superior went out with another friend"; "Why should I obey him or her; he or she doesn't really care about me." Obedience here is for what I get out of it from the other person for my own identity or self-esteem. There cannot be a growth in obedience without a serious and painful interior struggle out of and away from identification with mother or father figures of the past. The Lord must come to be the only one who sustains us, when we are "just and walk in the way of His commands."

3. Dependency

An outgrowth of non-internalizing identification (or rather, an underlying need which is at its source) is that of dependency. It can happen that one obeys because of the support, the care, the concern, the attention one can get from a superior. It may even come to the point where the superior becomes the one who eventually makes all or most of the decisions for the individual, debilitating the person's own human autonomy, while the superior feels "important," "necessary," "worthwhile." This is mutual dependency rather than a cooperative venture into discerning God's will to be lived autonomously according to the call of the Spirit in each, even in community life. Thus, though everyone sits in the community room watching TV, all may not be "obeying." Underlying motives, such as dependency, are possible so that I may be there because *he* or *she* is there, not because *God* is there. Rahner, speaking of this sort of thing, says: "Yet there can be no subordination of the individual to a community and to the authority representing it, if it tries to make the individual an exclusively dependent function of the community and its authority."[85]

4. Mistrust

From what do dependency and non-internalizing identification stem and to what do they lead? Mistrust: of *oneself*, of one's capacities for reasoning, for standing on one's own feet, for altruistic love; of *others*, of their genuine receptivity and willingness to live in mutual dialogue, awe, and discernment of God's workings and requests in each other. John Paul II writes: ". . . there is a marked lack of sensitivity and concern for others; fostering one's own career (ideas) at other people's expense; undermining one another's position; a widespread sense of mistrust. Instead of community spirit there is increasing social atomization . . . it is not only the walls that separate them, it is the whole atmosphere of distrust, indifference, and alienation. In such an atmosphere the human heart withers." He was speaking here of policies of the Communist Party regarding events in Poland—yet how realistic even in religious life![86] In mistrust then, in seeking to hide one another's limitations in separate "camps," we are not allowing ourselves to be open to the power of obediential love in each other. We do not allow ourselves to wish to be open to the other, available to be "helped toward God," if others objectively feel we are missing this.

> Even in cases where one tries to hide a shortcoming for which one is actually responsible, so that its becoming manifest would justifiably evoke in one a sense of painful humiliation, the desire to keep that secret quiet *at all costs* betrays a certain inner unfreedom. A true Christian will accept even this highly unpleasant kind of penance should his consideration for some important value (love, honesty, relationship, the Kingdom, obedience) demand it. But, above all, he will never allow his dread of shame to become the paramount factor dominating his inner life. For he knows that the wrong he may have committed is an evil merely for the reason that it offends God, and in comparison to that, the "disgrace" means nothing . . .[87]

If obedience means being open to grow in the will of the Father for us even through each other, we must have the courage to be willing to be human, letting our limits be made available to the gentle whispering of "come away from yourself," to the Spirit within each of us. We need, as a community, to help each other develop a healthier personal self-esteem, trusting more in the power of the virtues infused into each soul, and living in the Holy Spirit. This is a grave responsibility. Mistrust is built on fear, and fear, unfortunately, at times is justified because of facts— sometimes quite objectively, sometimes involving exaggeration.

Have we helped one another to trust by trusting others, by providing an atmosphere of genuine, warm receptivity where others will want to come to discern, to listen to God's plan with us?

5. Domination

A difficulty or abuse of obedience can be seen, at times, in the rigid, obsessive commands issued constantly from a determined, convinced, inflexible superior—or subject! How often we see leaders—"big leaders" or "little leaders"—telling everyone what to do, when to do it, how to do it, how often, and then insisting they come back to report if it has been done, when, why that way, etc. Some persons are dominated interiorly by an instinct for power;[88] and I do not mean only leaders! These people cannot accept limits to their authority. There are some who constantly insist the superior "should have done it that way," "could have been more gentle," "could have been more firm," "should have invited Father," "should not have invited Father," etc., etc.!! If the superior says yes and does one thing, that is a failure; if the superior does the opposite, it is a failure again! Perhaps these religious who always claim to know what real, mature obedience is in every situation, are more moved by power needs than by a gentle openness and listening to what God wants to do in their own lives. Just a note here: domination can also be seen in those who insist that everyone march to the same drummer, on the same path. Those who insist on conformity always forget one important fact: not all community members have the same gifts of the Holy Spirit. "Each one has his own gift of God, one in one way, another in another" (1 Cor 7:7; 12:8-11). To one is given the gift of wisdom, to another faith, to another knowledge, to another healing . . . If the need to dominate takes over, this theological, dynamic reality and value of the gifts of the Spirit will recede— although God calls us to common life and obedience in community, He seeks to do this by reaching our personal hearts, in love. Violence is done to our freedom and to our mature capacity to obey when coercion is used. Coercion can be applied crudely by physical threats or subtly by psychological pressure, manipulation or moral constraint. Obedience should flow from, and be accompanied by, a renunciation of egoism, an unconditional yes to follow Jesus in His obedience unto death.

6. *Dishonesty in Dialogue*

If passionate love for God, mutual responsibility and co-responsibility are the essential prerequisites for mature obedience through dialogue, it is essential that this dialogue or discussion be absolutely honest. Each must put their cards on the table, speaking the naked truth—all of it, not half-truths, or with emphasis put on certain aspects with essentials glossed over. Dialogue must be open—without subtle attempts to hear what one wants to hear or to prolong a decision or to tire the superior to the point where he or she will say, "OK. Have it your way!" Open dialogue does not mean trying to pit the superior against others, or to attempt to block every decision that is being made. Rather, in humility and truth, both superior and subject are called to search *disinterestedly* for the will of God, for the best means to actualize His will, the means most adapted for *that* person in *that* case. It should be a mutual discernment in a common project of love, not a way of ambiguity and distortion to maintain one's own will.

7. *Harm Avoidance*

Obedience can be *used* rather than *lived*, if an underlying subconscious need of harm avoidance directs much of one's life. If obedience becomes a passive submission to others' decisions, an execution of acts without an interiorized motive, only to "keep peace" and avoid harm to oneself, then there is no real autonomy existing. It is, rather, infantilism. Here, one cannot take the initiative for fear of making a mistake, or for fear of criticism, or for fear of one's own security. Those who act this way become the "nesters" in religious life; they enter into a stage of regulated mediocrity, avoiding excitement, searching for a smooth, comfortable bureaucratic existence. Rahner describes it further: "We would be doing our duty and receiving our food in return, we would be contented and therefore not make any great claims on life. This is not what religious obedience really means. It (this mediocrity) is really the sacrifice of a value of central importance as an act of faith. . . . It would even be a *bad* sign, either for our spirit of asceticism or for our human authenticity, vitality and strength . . ."[89] Rueda also summarizes it nicely:

> The true danger is in fact not that those who are directed, reaching a mature age, become more exigent, but that they prefer to nest (install themselves) rather than progress. A less grave illness of a young one is to be naive and somewhat silly, expressing oneself in a torrent of words which is badly regulated; . . . But he who is more mature knows on the other hand, that he can make his nest very discreetly, closing himself in his own closet, seeking comfortably a manner of continuing to live in a faith which does not cost, in a prayer which does not stimulate, and even in a dialogue which does not compromise. He can arrive easily enough at not renouncing either God or the world, searching patiently the outline of his circle—to serve God and to live comfortably. Obviously he finishes by serving no one.[90]

8. Individualism

One may say at this point, that the only solution to these other trends—dependency, identification, compliance, etc.—is to be an individualist. But this, too, can be a distortion of obedience. If individualism means "discerning for oneself" according to one's own needs and interests and charisms, then it can easily be or become self-centeredness. Christ never disobeyed by proclaiming an individualist conscience, by proclaiming His own right to autonomy, not even insofar as He claimed to be an echo of the voice of God. Rather, basing Himself on the Old Testament, and obeying the "true intimate destiny of the synagogue, of the chosen people, presented and announced in the Scriptures," He claimed only fulfillment of the Law, of the Covenant. "I have come not to destroy the Law, but to bring it to its completion." This was obedience and NOT rebellion (Mk 15:28; Lk 24:27, 32).[91] Thus, while one may claim to be an individualist, and believe this to be mature obedience, a listening to the Spirit speaking in oneself, we must recall that in each of us there is the possibility of inconsistencies and underlying motives (unconscious) which color this proclaimed value. Thus, our individualism may be a withdrawal or rationalization arising from mistrust, anger or hurt. No such withdrawal or individualism can be "pawned off" as mature obedience.

C. Third Level

1. Self-Righteousness

Very often, an attitude of self-righteousness may easily be formed in regard to religious obedience. What does this mean? Perhaps, by the grace of God we are managing to be listeners to His word and doers of His plans; but if this is followed by an attitude of "I am better than he or she, because I wear black clothes, or am here for prayers daily, or here for every meeting, while he or she is not," then a legalistic, compliant attitude may be underlying the obediential act.

It is, for example, very easy to be "charitable" *at the expense of others*; i.e. as a practice of *our* virtue, for *our* sanctified vision of ourselves. Then, at the moment, a practiced vow or virtue becomes an act of mere self-worth (it ceases to be charity!). The genuine vow or virtue is rather an expression of love for the other in God and for God in them (cf. 1 Jn 3:23-24), with the love and reverence and obedience *which Christ Himself bears them*. If we love or obey because the other is appealing and "thinks like I do"—that is, to imply that my own ways of thinking, my own ideals, are better than others'—then this is self-righteousness. It is to want others to obey me, rather than the Spirit in them, the Spirit working in both of us as Community. It is to forget again the Spirit's variety of ways of working. It is ultimately a dead-end to my wish for an enriching obedience:

To insist that everyone else think like myself and become like myself is to impoverish myself—e.g. to try to force everyone to adopt my own type of devotions, or my own pet apostolic projects. For in preventing another from being his own true self, in hampering the development of his own personality and special inclinations of grace, I am impoverishing the community. For I, too am most myself only in community, filling up by my own special developments in grace what is wanting in others, while they, by their graces and virtues, make up for what is wanting in me.[92]

Let us be aware that "piety" (and obedience too,) can mask hard-heartedness, indifference and bitterness, even inhumanity, if it is not open to the beauty of the "Fiat" of others, whispered in the intimate relation of each personal soul to God. To experience oneself as obedient is one thing, but to understand and interpret it in ourselves or in another is quite another thing.[93] As one author puts it: "some 'pious souls' drink avidly the cup of maudlin devotions while indulging their own sweet will, and shutting their hearts upon the neighbor."[94] This is not openness in love to serve the Spirit of God in the needs of others. It is imposing on them *our own* wills.

2. *Narcissism-Pride*

"Often today, under the affirmation of autonomous initiative and to counteract the 'passivity' of obedience, there is hidden the development of an inordinate pride, and non-dominated passion."[95] A narcissist is one who is in love with himself or herself—his or her own plans, his or her own visions, his or her own body, his or her own ideas. Narcissists will *use* the vow of obedience either 1) as superiors, to fulfill their own plans and visions and to prove how wonderful they are, or 2) as subjects, to exhibit their rights and their merits in order to obtain "permissions" to continue on in their own expectations of achievement for themselves. Their motto unconsciously is: "We are proud of ourselves, not proud of the Lord" (1 Cor 1:31). Both the self-righteous and the narcissists tend to compare what others do to their *own* accomplishments, and vice versa, esteeming themselves generally better than others. The self-righteous, on the one hand, could be satisfied to maintain their "obedience" in a circumscribed area, or within confined limits. Narcissists, in contrast, can easily seek to "use" the community for their own grandiose, endless plans—they are unable silently, humbly, and quietly to discern what is to be done, and they fall to pieces if someone asks a question regarding their "tactics" of obedience.

3. Absence of Faith

One vital component is lacking in the narcissist's "obedience"—that humble, awesome *vision of love* which comes from a deep inner fount of experience of one's *limitedness*,[96] and thus of the concomitant need for others—for community, for discernment, for God. We have *no* plans that are not *His*. We have no life that is not *His*—but we need to discern objectively that they *are* His. "By their fruits you shall know them . . ." In the genuine experience and assimilation of our own limitedness, God bends down with His loving gift of grace, and carries us on in *faith*. Faith is the assurance that God exists in every movement of our being, in every person, in every event; that He is sustaining us in His alliance and bringing it to completion. Any project or plan undertaken outside of or without a profound spirit of faith is merely human. It is not the surrender of the counsel of obedience.

4. Denial

a. Denial of the Ends of the Institute

The vow of obedience is made to God through the Church; however, it is made in a particular community, with its own charism and concrete ends. If a religious sister, of her own will and without the approval and permission of her own superiors, directs her efforts and existence to any goal outside these ends of the Institute, she is no longer following the vow of obedience as taken by her on the day of her profession. By "ends" of the Institute I do not mean only its "works." The goals or ends (e.g. sanctification, evangelization) and the means to reach these goals (including the "works" of the community) are prescribed by the Institute. Both ends and means should be a *lived* existential reality, for motives (as mentioned earlier) of the Lord alone. Misunderstandings, abuses and resistances may be the fruit of an incomplete or distorted vision of the Institute's goals, which are, in the final analysis, one: participation in the oblation of Christ.[97]

b. Denial of the Commitment taken in Religious Life

The commitment made on the day of our final consecration is a commitment made to "a community of persons consecrated to a common project of Christian sanctity, for evangelical witness and apostolic mission" for the good of the Universal Church.[98] A distortion of obedience occurs when one claims to obey for any other reasons, such as "Canon Law prescribes it so," or "the norms are wise," or "they help to regulate a good community life," or "the Church wants it so," or "people like it that way," or "the hierarchy arranged it so," or "so we can grow in self-control," etc. These reasons tend to be based only on partial truths—possibly more exclusively on the merely *human* levels in us. Here obedience loses the richness of its full dimension in Christ; commitment is narrowed.

c. Denial of the Reasons of the Law's Being

Simple distortions in understanding or living the counsel of obedience may occur from a denial of the *reasons* why there are rules and constitutions. As we recall from our study of the natural laws, each "law" is meant to facilitate growth on another level, for transcendence, as well as for the proper functioning of the whole. The Christian "law," however, goes beyond this to a "law of love," not merely the functional or utilitarian necessity of law. Religious, as we noted, look for guidance in their frailty and weakness, for means of expressing faith and love in the "laws" of religious life. The "laws" exist not for human reasons only, but to free one from oneself; even more, to be on that level of love which has its limits only in the eternal love of union with the Father.

5. *Rationalization*

Abuses of the vow of obedience can come about easily by the use of a defense commonly known as "rationalization." Rationalization is an attempt to explain away, or give reasons for one's behavior in an exteriorly acceptable manner. It is a "defense" because the reasons given are subconsciously meant to cover over less acceptable or less noble underlying processes. What kind of rationalizations do we hear, on occasion, regarding obedience? How is "obedience" used as a rationalization? The following examples will help: "The superior gave me permission and money to go—it is not *against* obedience!" This is not to say it *is* obedient, however, since obedience is a listening to God's call and plan in our own lives: is He calling to the cross and renunciation or to constant self-indulgence? "The superior said I could have this car of my own—I got permission." This is to avoid the fact that what is lawful may not always be prudent (for scandal, etc.), and prudence is as much a sensitivity to God's willed presence in humanness as is direct obedience.

"I was obedient—I went to the meeting—even if I wasted a day and I could have gotten much more done at home for school." This person calls it obedience, rationalizing an attitude of aggression and disapproval of the superior's commands by "pretending" to have had better things to do at home. Actually, obedience should include not merely external execution, but submission of will and submission of judgment (cf. St. Ignatius Loyola). "They call me a complainer, but actually I'm only being 'obedient,' trying to help the superior see what should be done more effectively for the community, being cooperative and helpful." This is a rationalization: "obedience" is being used to cover one's self-righteous aggression.

"I didn't obey because he or she said it so harshly; it wasn't necessary to be so strong . . ." Another rationalization; neglect of obedience is used to "pay back" the superior for his or her harshness—to throw the blame on him or her, while covering up one's own wish to be coddled and treated specially.

"His command was absurd, and we don't have to obey illogical commands." Rationalization? If the superior was unsympathetic to the subject's ideas (he calls it "illogical"), he does not obey; he rationalizes his own self-righteousness, and looks for reasons to say it is ridiculous, rather than trying to understand the meaning of the command. "I am involved in this thing because this is what the Church wants; it is following the 'signs of the times.' " Rationalization: he or she gives supposedly good reasons for possibly gratifying his or her own needs underneath. Has he or she really discerned the usefulness of the current trends as related to Gospel values? Is he or she confusing "signs of the times" with "axiological decadence," i.e. abandonment of fundamental values?[99] In a word, with Brother Rueda, we can see that: "if we want to rationalize the will of God to the point that our tiny idea of our tiny good is the measure and criterion by which to discern *His* will, then we are wasting our time."[100]

6. Jealousy

Very often we hear it said: he or she can go here, have this, do that, "get away" with this; and here am I, having to "toe the line!" This type of comment reveals a bitterness and egocentrism, a disgust with obedience, and an out-of-touch-ness with the essential meaning of the will of God for *me*. When we need to lower ourselves to compare ourselves with others, then the law of *love* brought to us by Christ—"for I give you a new law . . . not an eye for an eye or a tooth for a tooth . . ."—has been lost. Obedience is then empty. Our human plans and needs and inconsistencies, our depleted self-esteem and self-dissatisfaction are turned outward to attack others. Hinnebusch says: "As a man is, so he judges; to a fevered tongue, everything tastes bitter."[101] We come to judge others by our own depreciated standards. Because we may find community life or obedience burdensome, or feel inadequate to the task and want to escape, we project this smallness and limitedness into our idea of obedience and into the motives and acts of others. We leave no room for their own responsibility and do not take seriously their depth of spiritual life and living obedience. Because we really, inside, want a life of ease and comfort and do not want to bear our own share in the Cross of Christ—even to death—we presume others are doing the same. We make the other into ourselves. If we are not intimately secure in Jesus' daily personal love and presence and support, obedience becomes a response to structure, to rule, to obligation, to duty, rather than to a PERSON whom we love. If we have truly fallen in love with Jesus, and He is our all, and we are convinced of His burning love for us personally, what more do we need? Why must we make others the footstool of our insecurity and inferiority within? "Thou shalt not covet" also refers to our tendency to want to be like God (according to Fr. Lyonnet).[102] To want everything that everyone else has or is or does, is to want to be like God; this is pride, the first sin. It is not obedience!

So we have said there must be a solid structure of integrated needs and attitudes underneath before we can objectively discern what is God's will, alone and/or with others. We must all be aware of a few important psychological realities basic to the supernatural effectiveness of grace:

1. We may consciously will the end, e.g. obedience, but may not consciously will the means, e.g. following suggestions, events, etc. So, conscious willing of ends is not the same as, nor a guarantee of, conscious willing of the means.

2. We may consciously will the end (e.g. to be obedient) and also consciously will the means (e.g. to live the Constitutions in a spirit of love) but we may not be available *subconsciously* to will either the ends or the means—because of domination, dependency, exhibition, etc. Thus, making conscious the unconscious may be one of the chief tasks of morality and education. Conscious willing of ends and means does not guarantee subconscious willing of ends and means.[103]

We must be aware that within us we have "the oppressor and the oppressed," and that we need to be educated to discern, to alienate ourselves from whatever is inauthentic to a total "Fiat" to His movement of love in our lives.

In summary, we must remember that when the grace of God first lays hold of a person, it lives and develops first of all in those areas where there are no special defects to impede it and where there are certain good natural tendencies congenial to grace.[104] Genuine spiritual progress can be made in those areas long before grace has extended its influence into the other areas where there are obstacles, or where there is no special natural bent to be supernaturalized. *Once* the person has achieved a position of strength in that area, then he is able to work to extend the Kingdom of God, the influence of grace, to other areas of his personality.

Now the question arises as to how to grow out of this human natural limitation—how to open the other areas of one's personality to the workings of grace, if possible. Our wish to grow and deepen our obedience is already in itself an obedience—a response to the invitation: "Sell what you have and come, follow me."

VII. MEANS FOR GROWTH IN OBEDIENCE

As we near the end of this study, we raise a most important question: What can I do to help facilitate the workings of grace, the living of the counsel of obedience, in my life? A few practical suggestions are given here, but by the loving initiative and power of the Holy Spirit in each of us, many more will surface in our reflective moments.

A. Strengthen the Will

Mature obedience requires a determined effort to find God and surrender to His will in whatever difficult circumstances arise. It means that we must carry out and pursue this mission in long-term fidelity, in hard times and in glad, in clear vision as well as in confusion. This is not a mission for the wishy-washy. Obedience calls for single-mindedness and intense constancy of will, not merely in those situations which are exceptionally demanding or which lead in unusual directions, but also in the monotony of day-to-day and (to all appearances) insignificant surrenders.

Therefore, means should be taken day by day to maintain a strong will, flexible in its bending toward the greater good, the deeper command. How can this be done? Here are two ways:

1. Renunciation

As religious, we will never be able to renounce our will in large matters if we have not learned to say no to slighter desires and movements in our life, day by day. Each day simple things, on every level of being, present occasions for this "exercise" of the will: learning to say no to a harmless indulgence in some physical satisfaction—e.g. two pieces of candy instead of three; seven and a half hours of sleep instead of eight; one chapter read meditatively rather than three books rushed through; leaving the window closed when someone else closed it, though I'd prefer it opened; spending 45 minutes with a friend rather than two hours each day; accepting a TV program or radio station that is not my choice; living in uncertainty but following through on duties; in depressive moments, carrying on. Renunciation is redemptive in little things as well as in large; it fortifies the will for the cost of redemptive obedience in the larger sense. There are as many occasions for renunciation for the Kingdom, as there are for personal gratification. On the other hand, however, accepting a satisfying situation—a gift, a tender thought or generous service, an honor—may be a renunciation, a strengthening of will for other people. We need to renounce, thus, a radical autonomy or self-sufficiency, in this way too; we need to renounce the enclosures of our own determined world, to let others in as they may see fit, in God's plan.

2. Self-Forgetful Service

Another means to strengthen one's will for Christ is to make oneself available in a constant, stable manner to the needs of the Church, the community, the sister or brother next to me. This means willing the good of the other beyond my own; it means providing the loving support of Christ for the other person. Now, while it is difficult to serve *anyone*, how much *more* will it take to offer oneself to those who are less attractive, less appealing, less rewarding in their response. "Servants" will also be misunderstood and criticized, as was Christ. Can you *will* to remain near Him in service to His people even if depreciated and rejected and misjudged in your motives and goals? This is a strengthening of the will in God's loving, supportive grace. Difficult requests under more formal and obvious situations of obedience, then, will not leave us "faint of heart."

B. To Improve Our Discerning Process

If obedience includes dialogue, this presumes that we first actively discern what God calls us to in the events He allows or requests, and that we then present it for discernment to superiors. The same goes for superiors as regards their subjects, even if by obedience the final decision is left to the superior. How can the discerning process be improved? Here are some suggestions.

1. Clarifying Values

a. Christ's Values and One's Own Ideals

Often, difficulties in responding to God's plan in our daily life occur because, as time goes on, our ideals become (or remain) fuzzy. Our hierarchy of values becomes confused or reversed. Our interpretation of the Gospels becomes subjective. We become uncertain of our end, our goal. Therefore the "yes" of the counsel of obedience becomes meaningless or burdensome. But how to clarify my ideals? By taking time regularly for deep reflection—in time of retreat certainly, but not merely then. By keeping abreast of theological, objective interpretations of the Gospels (sanctioned by the Church), and seeking to find ways of implementing these values of Christ in my concrete living. An example may help to clarify this. Often we begin to rationalize our own behavior and tendencies by "quoting the Gospel" to an inquiring superior. If asked to discern why we go each week to such and such a person's house, we say: "Christ had His Bethany." This is a subjective interpretation: that Christ went to Bethany primarily to relax and be loved. The objective interpretation would be that Christ went to *teach* primarily, and incidentally did not go alone or all that regularly. Mary chose the "better part" not because she sat at His feet consoling Him, but because she sought to learn of God in simplicity and truth. Thus, our ideals should be clarified and articulated in a precise way: *What are we about?* Where are we going? Why are we doing this? For Christ, or for us? Is this the value of Christ?

b. Institutional Ideals

The community, too, seeks to clarify its own goals and ends. These ideals are presented clearly in the Constitutions, and are offered for further study and more precise understanding in classes, suggested readings, proposed discussions, and letters of the major superior. Taking these points for serious consideration can help clarify and energize one's life according to mutually held ideals. It would also be useful to look often at one's own ideals, the Gospel call, and the institutional call (the meaning of obedience), to see if all three "wills" are consonant. Consistency in ideals helps make and keep them more forceful in our lives.

2. Prayer and Meditation

If we are to progress in discernment, in dialogue and in surrender, then we must be prayerful, meditative people. Why? It is only after we have "dialogued" with the Lord in the profound, naked truth of what we are together, He and I, that we can say something valuable in exterior dialogue. Otherwise, the *source* of dialogue is simply the "human" me or the "intellectualized" Jesus . . . with no root or substance within. Dialogue then becomes empty; discernment distorted. Prayer, companionship with God, keeps His mind and goals and wishes ever before us, real, present and concrete. No surprises will occur then, when God asks something difficult in surrender to His plan. We can more easily situate it in His designs, because we are closely associated and acquainted with them. We learn to surrender ourselves as Jesus did, by meditating on His obedience to the Father. We must provide a desert for meditation and reflection, or a Bethany of study for reflective purposes. We must become other Marys of Bethany to know Him more clearly, other Marys of Nazareth to follow Him more intimately.

C. Teach Self to Listen

If we are to hear God in the Gospels, in the Church, in the community, in superiors—if we are to dialogue—then we must be able to listen. What can we do to expand our capacity to *listen*, to hear *objectively*? First of all, we can try to understand the presence, the experiences, the here-and-now of the *other*. That means holding off comparisons with self or making immediate, hasty interpretations after one sentence, one phrase, or one meeting. Slowly, with time and in peace, we can be available to see the world with their eyes, feel it with their heart. This does not mean to lose sight, however, of one's own—or God's own—vision, but rather to "put on" the other's sandals, to feel and experience their inner turmoil or peace, joy or pain, uncertainty or zeal; their ideals and needs and attitudes; and the synthesis of all of these in their own personal hierarchy. Understanding and listening may mean, at times, having to ask questions so as to be more objective and closer to truth, more supportive or more confronting. We must always have an attitude of humble awe as we listen to the other—awe at the mysterious and incomprehensible workings of Providence in each movement within the person. Thus, listening in itself becomes an "obedience"—a focusing on His workings and desires and requests in the here and now—a "finding God in all things," in all persons.

D. Keep the Spiritual Needs of the Universal Church in Mind

If the counsel of obedience is actualized for the sake of Christ, in and through His universal Church, then it is helpful to keep ourselves informed and aware of the struggles and goals and trends of the Church beyond the confines of our own inner self, our mission and our community.

1. In Its Hierarchical Structure

This means that it is useful to keep abreast of the interests of the hierarchy—following with openness, sincerity and docility the teachings, preachings and studies of the Pope, as well as those appointed to govern with him on a local level. An enlightened attitude of obedience to the universal Church is necessary before we can actualize this obedience more concretely in our local situation. Following the guidance of the hierarchy in its teaching or exhortative ministry, is an invaluable support for our being identified more closely with Christ in His appointed vicar. At the same time, it is a constant remedy for our own tendency towards shallowness or "telescoped" obedience.

2. In Its "Grass-Roots" Ministry

This openness to the Spirit working through hierarchical trends and exhortations, should be complemented by an interest in the workings and call of God right "in our own back yard." Are we eager to find what God is asking of us in the people on the street—the poor, the aged, the anxious, the confused, the depressed, the uncertain, the minorities—even those outside our immediate ministry? Are we open to listen to His requests, His inspirations, His presence in them? Are we ready to pray for them in genuine, profound concern? To sacrifice in obedience, seeing His Incarnation in them?

E. Keep the Needs of the Local Community in Mind

1. In Its Hierarchical Structure

When was the last time you wondered what you could do to alleviate the burdens of your general or local superior? Have you listened recently to the real meaning of their decisions, pondered them, sought Christ's workings in them? How often we forget that our own superiors, crucified in love with the Master, have a wisdom tempered by suffering and sensitivity, and a vision that spans not only themselves and us, but the Community and the Church as well. Mature religious express a spontaneous, loving obedience even in their *attitude toward* people in positions of authority. They do not expect them to be infallible, inexhaustible, super-human—in other words, "gods." We must recall that any higher office has such grave and vast responsibilities and demands that no single person (outside of God Himself) can have the fullness of all the qualities needed to fulfill the task totally and perfectly. Rahner puts it beautifully:

> The higher the office the smaller the possibility, humanly speaking, of fulfilling it. For we may reasonably presume that the degrees of variation in mental and moral gifts among men are less than the degrees of difficulty found in the management of various social enterprises. As a rule, therefore, more important duties will unavoidably be more poorly performed than lesser ones.
> Along with the assumption of a more important responsibility comes the painful realization, felt both by the superior and those about him, that the man is far from being equipped for his task. The defective fulfillment of higher obligations cruelly lays bare the shortcomings of a man's capacities which previously escaped our attention.[105]

Since superiors are weak and limited in this sense—as are all of us—there is need for the counsel of obedience based on faith. Our heartfelt participation in the cross which they so generously offered to bear for us, can best be actualized in our honesty, sincerity and availability to be with them, out of love for the Church. We are participants with them in zeal for the Church, in genuine love and support for each other, in our willingness to discern with them in humility, and to leave to them in faith and trust the final presentation of what is seen to be the greatest good for fulfilling the plan of the Master in our lives. Promptness and stability in carrying out our mission is part of our cooperation with them in building up His Body. Thus we need to cultivate a spirit of openness and understanding towards them, and of co-responsibility with them. We need to see them as persons, not as magistrates; as sisters or brothers seeking together with us God's will for our own good and that of the Church.

2. In Its "Grass-Roots" Ministry

The needs of the local community in each house, each "department," each ministry, should be the concern of all, not in a critical, judgmental way, but in a supportive, enthusiastic manner. Sharing what is happening in our own area—the funny episodes, the delicate moments, the worries and difficulties involved in our own personal living-out of obedience—is a simple way of mutually inspiring, informing and challenging each other to see the presence of the Lord in the events of each day. Very often our own obedience becomes egocentric and closed-in because we have not found the joy of sharing in the obediences of others. We do not understand or perceive fully what good is being done for the Church in the quiet, unassuming apostolates of others.

F. Keep the Needs of the Whole Individual in Mind

1. Their Spiritual Well-Being

Finally, we come to the most concrete expression of obedience—our obediential reverence for the work of the Spirit in each other. How much we need to cultivate an attitude of genuine fraternal interest and love and delicate support of the growth of the Lord in each sister and brother! We stop short of the real meaning of community when we concentrate on exteriors—where one is, how one dresses, talks, walks, etc. We tend to forget the real interior needs of the individual, the *spirit* of each one. Can we support their zeal, touch their spirits of abandonment and courage and hope with our own spiritual gifts, whatever they be—gifts of peace and gentleness, humor and wisdom, interior struggle and pain? The most beautiful gift we can give each other in mutual obedience is the gift of a heart struggling to know Him more fully and surrender more completely in every facet of our existence. We call each other, as the disciples were called, to listen, to respond, to surrender, to find Him where we least expect Him in our lives—and we teach others how to do this. The most beautiful, tender expression of a mature obedience can be a whispered "I said a Hail Mary for you," or "I'll remember you at Mass," or "I offered these pains for your work and your continued spirit," or "I'll meet you at the Eucharist," or a simple "Thank God and you—He is with you closely!"

2. Their Humanness

If we are at peace with God's gifts in our own being, and awed by what God is doing in us, sensitive to our failures and insecurities and questions, joys and successes, hopes and visions—with all of our "humanness" on every level—then we will be much more sensitive also to our own realistic limitations. When we accept and struggle with these, we will be more in touch with the same in others. We must trust that we are *all* struggling to rid ourselves of inhibiting, cramping factors within us which color or distort God's voice—rebellion against directives; the search for comfort or unhindered freedom; fear of responsibility; obstinacy, aggressiveness. Yet we need to be willing to "stick our necks out" and gently discuss these with others when they appear, in a loving, concerned way for them as individuals. We cannot do this with a self-righteous, dominating attitude of "You don't measure up to my standards, so get to it!" Understanding the needs of the individual is more than merely being sensitive to the others' struggles to be open to God's voice. It is also to confirm and evoke those positive, blessed gifts of the Spirit (and even the human ones) already at work in them, by which they are responding to God's voice and call. It is to be available for support, to rejoice with them, to recognize the human qualities with which they have gifted His Kingdom. This means, in obediential love, to make ourselves available to "complement" them, to be a fulfilling, cooperating person (where possible) in spontaneous service. But how to do this? To the one who has difficulty in sewing, an offer of assistance from a "seamstress"; to the one unclear about "where she is going" personally, an offer of counsel; to the one who feels a "klutz" in cooking, a helping hand or explanation; to one who is finding study particularly hard, the sharing of one's own knowledge. How many hundreds of ways in daily concrete situations we can grow in obedience with each other! No one individual has all things or can do all things. It is the very essence of limitedness that leaves room for our response of love in obedience to what the Spirit asks of us through the other. What a masterpiece of design is this Mystical Body which we are called to develop through the specific treasures and limits and needs of each of us as individual human beings! Is there anything we wouldn't do for Jesus were He here in person? Would we wait to be asked by Him to do it if we were really madly in love with Him? And yet, the "Word became Flesh, and dwells among us," in our brothers and sisters.

VIII. CONCLUSION

How much more could be said regarding obedience? How complex it is to understand, yet how simple. As we seek a model for this simplicity of total surrender in love, we can consider the example of Mary.

The Story of Obedience

Christ		Mary
Nativity	"let what you have said be done to me"	Fiat
Crucifixion	"into Your hands I commend my spirit"	Pieta
Resurrection	"I return to the Father"	Assumption

Mary is the Virgin who ever listens in prayer. Mary accepts the invitation she hears and submerges herself in a faith and dialogue which we can call "active and responsible obedience." Mary is the Virgin Mother, the Virgin who offers. She is above all the model of those who make of their lives an offering to God. Her "yes" is, for all Christians, a lesson and an example of how to make of obedience to the will of the Father, the way and the means of one's own sanctification.[106]

Mary's obedience is the concrete expression of the unqualified response that she made in love: a response that was so deep and total that it was eternally faithful. It was never to be withdrawn, even when it led her to Calvary. She knew that obedience must be an effective readiness to let herself be conformed to the Lord Jesus even in His Passion.

Mary yearned, with a consuming intensity, to find Him again, in the full light of eternity, beyond all possibility of ever again being separated; she was assumed into heaven.

The Mother of the Lord, Mary, remained always perfectly transparent to God's word; hers was a perfect acceptance of Him, an ardent, ever faithful living will to be with Him, like Him, for Him.

Her love, like the immensity of her desires, was completely fulfilled. In her, the extension of the Lord's Resurrection was accomplished even in her body, to remain for us a living image of what the entire Church—what *we*—are called to become when we will have brought to fullness the mystery of our own precious religious obedience in Christ.[107]

With her, again and again, and with renewed fervor and hope, in each moment of our obediential love, we pray:

> Take, O Lord, and receive my entire life:
>   my memory,
>   my understanding,
>   my whole will.
> All that I am and all I possess
>   you have given me.
> I surrender it all to you
>   to be disposed of
>   according to your will.
> Give me only your love and your grace,
>   with these I will be rich enough
>   and will desire nothing more.
>
> *St. Ignatius*

Footnotes

1. J. Nuttin, *Psychoanalysis and Personality. A Dynamic Theory of Normal Personality* (New York: New American Library, 1962), pp. 220ff.
2. Karol Wojtyla (John Paul II), *The Acting Person*, (Boston: D. Reidel Publ. Co., 1979). The first level of being is extensively considered and treated on pp. 196-219.
3. Wojtyla, ibid. (especially pp. 206-210) makes a necessary distinction between feeling or emotivity and reactivity at this level: "Reactivity, a characteristic trait of the human soma related to the external mobility of the body is constituted from the specific raw material of the action." For example, a level of oxygen in the body recedes, and the body "reacts" by searching for air. On the other hand, "the ability to feel" at this bodily level consists also in the reception of stimuli coming from material sources; however their effect is not merely somatic (e.g. consisting, say, in a movement of the body); rather—or in addition—there is a physical effect expressed in "feelings" which transcend the mere body-reaction. For example, the level of oxygen recedes, one "feels" faint, or cold, or suffocating; one searches for air.
4. Ibid., p. 272.
5. Ibid., pp. 223-224.
6. Karl Rahner, "Reflections on the Theology of Renunciation," in *Theological Investigations*, Vol. III, (New York: Seabury Press, 1977), p. 54.
7. Nuttin, p. 223.
8. L. Suenens, "Obbedienza e Fedeltà," in Karl Rahner et al., *Nuovo Stile di Obbedienza*, (Milan: Ancora, 1969), p. 266.
9. Michel Labourdette, "Il Bene Comune come Fondamento dell' Obbedienza," in Rahner et al., p. 38.
10. For a relevant discussion of friendship and interpersonal relationships along this line, consult: Wojtyla, p. 176.
11. For the lengthier distinctions between rational and emotional appraisal, see L.M. Rulla, *Depth Psychology and Vocation*, (Rome: Gregorian University Press, and Chicago: Loyola University Press, 1971), pp. 31-34; B. Kiely, *Psychology and Moral Theology*, (Rome: Gregorian University Press, 1980), pp. 131-136. Both rely heavily on the works of Magda Arnold: M.B. Arnold, *Emotion and Personality*, 2 vols., (New York: Columbia University Press, 1960) and Magda Arnold (Ed.), *Feelings and Emotions. The Loyola Symposium*, (New York-London: Academic Press, 1970).
12. Nuttin, p. 223.
13. Wojtyla, p. 115.
14. Wojtyla's treatment of emotion, pp. 232ff. is very enlightening. He explains the various types of emotion possible on each level, and the possibility of "transformation" of these levels.
15. The "higher man" Wojtyla describes as he who manifests himself in the experience of both transcendence and integration: the "lower man" as he who, because of the transcendence appropriate to the action of a person, still requires integration, p. 255.
16. Ibid., p. 226.

17. Dietrich von Hildebrand, *Transformation in Christ*, (New York: Image Books, 1963), p. 189. Note also Wojtyla's deeply philosophical discussion of the "spiritual" level and integration of levels in transcendence on pp. 178-187 of *The Acting Person*.

18. P. Dezza, "Obbedienza e Spirito di Iniziativa," in Rahner et al., p. 281.

19. The same is also found in the *Pastoral Constitution on the Church in the Modern World, Gaudium et Spes*, no. 22.

20. B. Rueda, *Eccomi Signore. Conversazioni sull'Obbedienza*, (Rome-Milan: Ancora, 1975), p. 36.

21. Peter Fransen, *The New Life of Grace*, (New York: Seabury Press, 1973), p. 112.

22. Ibid., p. 135.

23. Rahner, "Cristo Modello dell'Obbedienza Sacerdotale," in Rahner et al., pp. 21, 25.

24. Giuseppe O. Girardi, *La Vita Religiosa, 1 Teologia della Vita Religiosa*, (Naples: Edizioni Dehoniane, 1979), p. 108. For a masterly treatment of the relation between obedience, both Christian and Religious, and the Will of God, drawing on the Patristic tradition, see: Irenée Hausherr, "The Will of God and Christian Obedience," *The Way Supplement*, 5 Feb. 1968, the entire supplement.

25. Rueda, p. 89.

26. Rahner, "Cristo Modello dell'Obbedienza Sacerdotale," p. 15.

27. Rahner, "The Priest and His Superiors," in *Meditations on the Priestly Life*, (London: Sheed and Ward, 1970), p. 131.

28. Rahner, "Reflections on the Theology of Renunciation," p. 54; "The Passion and Asceticism," p. 83, in *Theological Investigations*, Vol. III.

29. Michel Labourdette, "Il Bene Comune come Fondamento dell'Obbedienza," in: Rahner et al., p. 43.

30. Paul Hinnebusch, *Salvation History and the Religious Life*, (Denville, New Jersey: Dimension Books, 1966), p. 196.

31. Ignace de la Potterie, "Christ's Obedience: Basis and Model of Christian Obedience," in: *Obedience: Christian, Religious, Jesuit*, (Rome: Centrum Ignatianum Spiritualitatis, 1980), p. 17.

32. David M. Knight, *Cloud by Day, Fire by Night*, Vol. III (Denville, New Jersey: Dimension Books, 1979). As regards "antecedent will," Knight writes: "This refers to what God desires, what He wants done, prior to any decision or command of the superior" (p. 67). This is different from the consequent will: "this refers to what God wants done, what His real will is for the subject *after* the superior has made his decision and spoken with authority" (p. 67). It is to be recalled that there may be at times an inconsistency between the two, not because God's will is inconsistent, but because of man who interprets it (singularly as subject as regards "antecedent will" and as superior as regards the "consequent will")—recall the subconscious inconsistencies which are part of human nature and the pervasive unconscious needs which may color man's interpretation of values and of God's will. L.M. Rulla, *Depth Psychology and Vocation*, 1971; Rulla, Ridick, Imoda, *Entering and Leaving Vocation*, 1976; B. Kiely, *Psychology and Moral Theology*, 1980; Ridick, "Value Orientation and Discernment," *Review for Religious*, 1976, 35, 914-927; Rulla, "The Discernment of Spirits and Christian Anthropology," *Gregorianum 59*, 1978,

537-569; Rulla, "Psicologia e Formazione Sacerdotale: premesse per un dialogo," *Seminarium*, July-September 1978, 438-459; Rulla, "Freedom and Discipline in Religious Formation, some anthropological considerations," *Proceedings of the 15th National Assembly, National Conference of Vicars for Religious.* Rome, March 14-22, 1981. (Buffalo, N.Y.), pp. 32-43.

33. *Lumen Gentium*, no. 31.
34. *Perfectae Caritatis*, no. 14.
35. Thomas Aquinas, *Summa Theologiae*, 2a 2ae, Q.44, a.4, ad 3.
36. John M. Lozano, *Discipleship: Toward an Understanding of Religious Life*, (Chicago: Claret Center for Resources in Spirituality, 1980), p. 221.
37. Hans Urs von Balthasar, *Vocazione*, (Rome: Rogate, 1981), pp. 32, 35, 40, 41, 48, 53.
38. John M. Lozano, "L'Obbedienza: Problemi Dottrinali e Tentativi di Soluzione," in: Koser et al., *Autorità e Obbedienza nella Vita Religiosa*, (Milan: Ancora, 1978), p. 186.
39. Atanasio Matanic, "Autorità e Obbedienza nella Vita e nella Spiritualità dei Religiosi da S. Francesco d'Assisi a S. Ignazio di Loyola," in Koser et al., pp. 106, 135-136; G.O. Girardi, pp. 47-67; *Evangelica Testificatio; Perfectae Caritatis*, nn. 1, 4, 5, 14. Rueda in *Eccomi Signore* says (p. 78): "The intensity of adherence to obedience is greater in the religious at least in the form of life and in existential projects. In him there is a condensation which from the beginning places all the life under obedience, whereas for Christians who are not religious this obedience is more dispersed, less decided in advance."
40. German Martel, "L'Esercizio Pastorale dell'Autorità," in: Rahner et al., p. 197.
41. Rueda, pp. 74-79.
42. Lozano, p. 248.
43. Hinnebusch, p. 108.
44. Dezza, p. 292.
45. Rahner, "Christ as the Exemplar of Clerical Obedience," in: *Obedience to the Church*, (Washington, D.C.: Corpus Books, 1969), pp. 1-2, 11. Also Rahner, "Cristo Modello dell'Obbedienza Sacerdotale," in Rahner et al., p. 24.
46. Stanislaus Lyonnet, "Autorità e Obbedienza alla Luce della Scrittura," in: Koser et al., p. 42.
47. Rahner, "Considerazioni Dogmatiche sulla Scienza e Coscienza di Cristo" *Saggi di Cristologie e di Mariologia* (Rome: Edizioni Paoline, 1965), pp. 199-238. Rahner presents an interesting evaluation of the relation between "knowledge of divine sonship" in Christ, and its gradual evolution as regards its objectivization.
48. *Lumen Gentium*, no. 42.
49. de la Potterie, pp. 13-14.
50. Rahner, "Some Reflections on Obedience," in R.W. Gleason, (Ed.) *Contemporary Spirituality* (New York: Macmillan, 1968), p. 134. Similar concepts are presented by G. Martelet, "The Church, Holiness and Religious Life," ibid., pp. 84-111.
51. Girardi, p. 116.
52. L. Gutierrez Vega, *Autoridad y Obbediencia en La Vida Religiosa*, (Madrid: Insituto Vida Religiosa, 1974), p. 125.

53. J.M.R. Tillard, "Autorité et Vie Religieuse," *NRTh 88*, 1966, 786-806. He says that religious authority is an ecclesial mystery, a service rendered to the group and to individuals as a help for discovering the will of God here and now.
54. Nuttin, p. 199.
55. Rahner, "The Passion and Asceticism," *Theological Investigations*, Vol. III, pp. 80-84.
56. Wojtyla, p. 131.
57. Rahner, "The Priest and His Superiors," *Meditations on Priestly Life*, (London: Sheed and Ward, 1970), pp. 124-125.
58. Girardi, p. 109.
59. Relevant readings regarding faith and obedience can also be had in: Matanic, pp. 134-136; Lozano, pp. 183ff.; Lyonnet, p. 56; de la Potterie, pp. 21, 22; Dezza, p. 295.
60. Rahner, "Theology of Freedom," in: *Theological Investigations*, Vol. VI, (New York: Seabury Press, 1969), p. 188.
61. Readings relevant to Mercy: John Paul II, *Dives in Misericordia*; Hinnebusch, p. 172.
62. John Paul II, *Dives in Misericordia*, n. 2.
63. *Dives in Misericordia*, passim; and *Gaudium et Spes* (Vatican II: Pastoral Constitution on the Church in the Modern World) no. 10 on the dichotomy within the human person.
64. Readings relevant to Humility: Encyclical on Priestly Celibacy, no. 70; Ph 2:6-13; Si 3:17-18, 20, 28-29.
65. Readings relevant to Justice: *Dives in Misericordia. The Way*. Vol. 13, July, 1973, the whole issue, pp. 171-228. Also see D. Nugent, "Justice, Love and Peace," *The Way*, 19, 4, 1979, pp. 283-291.
66. Von Hildebrand, pp. 256-272.
67. Readings relevant to Co-responsibility and Discernment: Girardi, pp. 119, 121, 126; Gino Corallo, "L'Educazione alla Obbedienza," in Rahner et al., p. 257; T. Goffi, "Rinnovamento delle Forme di Obbedienza nella Vita Religiosa," in Koser et al., p. 257; L. Bombin, "L'Obbedienza Religiosa nel Diritto Canonico," ibid., p. 331.
68. Rahner, "The Priest and His Superiors," p. 133.
69. As regards "unrealistic expectations" and the necessity for discernment, consult Rulla, Ridick, Imoda, 1976; Goffi, pp. 291, 294, 275-276; Bernard Lonergan, *Insight: A Study of Human Understanding*, revised students' edition, (London: Longmans Green, 1958), pp. 610-611.
70. Michel Pellegrino, "La Falsa Antinomia fra Autorità e Libertà" in Rahner et al., p. 160.
71. Some readings on the usefulness of Dialogue can be had in Jn 13:14-17; *Ecclesiam Suam*, nn. 51, 52, 55; and G. Martel, "L'Esercizio Pastorale dell'Autorità," in Rahner et al., pp. 214-215.
72. Readings on Valuing the Individual: Leo Suenens, "Obbedienza e Fedeltà," in: Rahner et al., p. 268; Karl Rahner, "Cristo Modello dell'Obbedienza Sacerdotale," in Rahner et al., p. 18; Girardi, p. 119.
73. Readings on the Common Good and Complementarity: Girardi, pp. 119-123; 1 Cor 10:26, 31-33.

74. Readings on Psychological Maturity: Rulla, *Depth Psychology and Vocation*; Rulla, Ridick, Imoda, op. cit.; Kiely, op. cit.; Barnabas Ahern, "Maturity: Christian Perfection," *The Way: Supplement*, 15, Spring, 1972, 3-16; "Christian Maturity and the Cross of Christ," *Proceedings of the Congress on the Wisdom of the Cross*, (Leumann-Torino: Elle-Di-Ci, 1975), II, 9-17; "Jesus, the Priest, Source and Model of Consecrated Service," *L'Osservatore Romano* (English Ed.), Sept. 2, 1976, 7-8; Italia Valle, "Persona, Comunità e Obbedienza: Problemi Psicologici," in Koser et al., p. 232.

75. Jane Loevinger, "Origins of Conscience," in M.M. Gill, and P.S. Holzman, Eds., *Psychology vs. Metapsychology. Psychoanalytic Essays in Memory of George Klein*, (N.Y.: International Universities Press, Psychological Issues), Volume IX, *14*, Monograph 36, 1976, pp. 289ff.

76. For a summary of Kohlberg's stages see: R. Duska & M. Whelan, *Moral Development: A Guide to Piaget and Kohlberg*, (Paramus, New Jersey: Paulist Press, 1975), pp. 45-47. See also: Kiely, pp. 50-62, 201-202; Dezza, p. 278; Corallo, pp. 248-249; Rulla, "Psicologia e formazione sacerdotale: premesse per un dialogo," pp. 438-439; Rulla, "Discernment of Spirits and Christian Anthropology," in Spidlik et al., *Ignatian Spirituality: Four Essays*, (Rome: Centrum Ignatianum Spiritualitatis, 1979), pp. 25-60.

77. For an excellent critique of Kohlberg and consideration of Loevinger's limits, see Kiely, *Psychology and Moral Theology*, (Rome: Gregorian University Press, 1980), pp. 109-112, 64-65, 75. See also, as regards Kohlberg: Paul C. Vitz, *Christian Moral Values and Dominant Psychological Theories: The Case of Kohlberg*, (New York University, 1983), and especially Vitz, "Secular Humanism and Morality," *The New Oxford Review*, July-August, 1981, pp. 12-16.

78. The works of Rulla, Ridick and Imoda are to be noted here as useful for pin-pointing underlying sources of difficulty in religious obedience.

79. Adrian Van Kaam, *The Transcendent Self*, (Denville, New Jersey: Dimension Books, 1979), p. 139.

80. Rulla, *Depth Psychology and Vocation*, pp. 150ff.; Rulla, Ridick and Imoda, pp. 115-120; H.C. Kelman, "Compliance, Identification and Internalization: three processes of attitude change," *Journal of Conflict Resolution*, 1958, *2*, pp. 51-60; "Three Processes of Social Influence," *Public Opinion Quarterly*, 1961, *25*, pp. 57-78; "Effects of Role-Orientation and Value-Orientation on the Nature of Attitude Change," paper read at East. Psychol. Assoc., New York, 1960.

81. Fransen, p. 121.

82. Rulla, Ridick, Imoda, pp. 116, 118, 120, 215, 237-238.

83. Fransen, p. 37.

84. Valle, p. 232.

85. Rahner, "Some Reflections on Obedience," in Gleason, pp. 126-128.

86. Sermon of K. Wojtyla, June 1978. In G. Blazynski, *Pope John Paul II*, (New York: Dell Publ., 1979).

87. Von Hildebrand, pp. 210-211.

88. Fransen, pp. 130-131.

89. Rahner, "The Priest and His Superiors," p. 129.

90. Rueda, p. 68.

91. Rahner, "Cristo Modello dell'Obbedienza Sacerdotale," in Rahner et al., p. 22.
92. Hinnebusch, p. 203.
93. Wojtyla, *The Acting Person*, p. 17.
94. Fransen, p. 304.
95. Dezza, p. 289.
96. For a clear discussion of limitations and acceptance of limits in oneself, see Kiely, pp. 23, 173-189, 199, 200-207, 276.
97. Girardi, p. 22.
98. Ibid.
99. Rueda, p. 87.
100. Ibid., p. 34.
101. Hinnebusch, p. 205.
102. Fransen, p. 116. Fransen discusses Lyonnet's explanation of Ch. 7 of the Letter to the Romans (Rm 7:7; Ex 20:17; Dt 5:21). By "covet," Paul did not mean sexual lust or desire, but the underlying nature of all sin: to want to be like God.
103. Note Wojtyla's discussion of the importance of the unconscious: *The Acting Person*, Chapter 2, paragraphs 7d, 7e. Also see relevant passages in *Analecta Husserliana, Vol. III, The Human Being in Action*, Anna Teresa Tymieniecka (Ed.), (Dordrecht, Holland: D. Reidel, 1978).
104. Hinnebusch, pp. 192-198.
105. Rahner, "Some Reflections on Obedience." In Gleason, pp. 124-125. Similar concepts are found in Rueda, pp. 98-99.
106. *Marialis Cultus*, nn. 7-20.
107. G. Pelland, "A Theological Reflection on Obedience," in *Obedience: Christian, Religious, Jesuit*, (Rome: Centrum Ignatianum Spiritualitatis, 1980), p. 30; Lk 1:38.

Bibliography

Abbott, W.M. (S.J.) Ed. *The Documents of Vatican II*. New York: Guild Press, 1966. (*Perfectae Caritatis*, no. 14).

Agnew, F.H. Obedience: A New Testament Reflection. In *Review for Religious*. 1980, 39, pp. 409-418.

Arnold, M.B. *Emotion and Personality*. 2 vols. New York: Columbia University Press, 1960.

Arnold, M.B. (Ed.). *Feelings and Emotions. The Loyola Symposium*. New York-London: Academic Press, 1970.

Clarke, T. (S.J.) *New Pentecost or New Passion? The Direction of Religious Life Today*. New York: Paulist Press, 1973.

Cusson, G. (S.J.) The Letter and the Spirit. Obedience, Authority and Spiritual Discernment. In *The Way. Supplement.* no. 36, 1979, pp. 82-99.

de Finance, J. (S.J.) L'atto morale e il soggetto. In *Rassegna di teologia.* 1972, 2, pp. 122-131.

de la Potterie, I. (S.J.). Christ's Obedience: Basis and Model of Christian Obedience. In *Obedience: Christian, Religious, Jesuit.* Rome, CIS, 1980.

Dictionnaire de Spiritualité. Paris: Beauchesne, 1981, pp. 535-564.

Farrell, W. (O.P.) *A Companion to the Summa.* New York: Sheed and Ward, 1952.

Flick, M. (S.J.), Alszeghy, Z. (S.J.) *Il mistero della croce.* Brescia: Queriniana, 1978.

Fowler, J. Theology and Psychology in the Study of Faith Development. In *Concilium.* New York: Seabury, 1982.

Fransen, P. (S.J.) *The New Life of Grace.* New York: Seabury Press, 1973, pp. 107-142; 231-245; 273-324.

Galot, J. (S.J.) I Consigli evangelici e l'impegno del Regno. In *Vita Consacrata.* 1977, 1, pp. 1-14.

Girardi, G.O. (S.C.J.) *Consacrazione: i consigli evangelici.* Rome: Edizioni Dehoniane, 1979.

Gleason, R.W. (S.J.) *Contemporary Spirituality.* New York: Macmillan Co., 1968.

Greene, T. (S.J.) *When the Well Runs Dry.* Notre Dame, Indiana: Ave Maria Press, 1978.

Guardini, R. Realismo Cristiano. In *Humanitas.* Brescia, 1975, pp. 95-101.

Haring, B. (C.Ss.R.) *Le Sacre et le Bien.* Paris: Editions Fleures, 1963 (Chapter IV).

Hausherr, I. (S.J.) The Will of God and Christian Obedience. In *The Way. Supplement.* February, 1968, pp. 5-68.

Healy, T. (S.J.) Human Freedom. Unpublished manuscript. Rome: Istituto Psicologia, PUG, April 1979.

Hinnebusch, P. (O.P.) *Salvation History and the Religious Life*. Denville, New Jersey: Dimension Books, 1966 (Chapters, 13, 21, 25, 26, 27, 28).

Hughes, A.C. *Preparing for Church Ministry. A Practical Guide to Spiritual Formation*. Denville, New Jersey: Dimension Books, 1979 (Chapter III).

Hughes, G.W. Formation for Freedom. In *The Way. Supplement*. 1977, 32, pp. 38-46.

Hughes L.M. Affectivity, Conscience and Christian Choice. In *The Way. Supplement*. 1975, 24, pp. 35-65.

Ignatius of Loyola, (St.) *The Letter on Obedience*. (William J. Young, S.J. Transl.) New York: America Press, 1953.

John Paul II (Karol Wojtyla), *The Acting Person*. Trans. by Andrzej Potocki. Boston: D. Reidel Publ. Co., 1979.

_____. *Dives in Misericordia*. Encyclical Letter on the Mercy of God. Boston: St. Paul Editions, 1980.

_____. *Love and Responsibility*. Trans. by H.T. Willetts. Glasgow: Collins Fount Paperbacks, 1982. New York: Farrer, Straus and Giroux, 1981.

_____. *Sign of Contradiction*. New York: Crossroad Publ. Co., 1980.

_____. The Structure of Self-Determination as the Core of the Theory of the Person. In: *Tommaso d'Aquino nel suo settimo centenario. Atti del Congresso Internazionale*. Naples: Edizioni Domenicane Italiane, 1974.

_____. Dalla croce di Gesù l'esempio dell'obbedienza. General Audience, *L'osservatore romano*. March 13, 1980, p. 1.

_____. Il Papa a religiosi e alle religiose. *L'osservatore romano*. February 4, 1981, pp. 1-2.

_____. La verità vi farà liberi. *L'osservatore romano*. April 16, 1981, p. 1.

Katz, D. The Functional Approach to the Study of Attitudes. In M. Fishbein, (Ed.) *Readings in Attitude Theory and Measurement.* New York: John Wiley and Sons, 1967.

Kiely, B. (S.J.). *Psychology and Moral Theology.* Rome: Gregorian University Press, 1980.

Knight, D.M. (S.J.) *Cloud by Day, Fire by Night.* Denville, New Jersey: Dimension Books, 1979. Vol. III .

Kohlberg, L. From Is to Ought: How to Commit the Naturalistic Fallacy and Get Away with It in the Study of Moral Development. In Miscel, T. (Ed.) *Cognitive Development and Epistemology.* New York: Academic Press, 1971.

_____. Education, Moral Development and Faith. In *Journal of Moral Education.* 1974, 4.

Kohlberg, L.; Turiel, P. Moral Development and Moral Education. In G. Lesser (Ed.) *Psychology and Educational Practice.* New York: Scott Foresman, 1971.

Kohlberg, L.; Colby, A.; Gibbs, J.; Speicher-Dubin, B.; Power, C. *Assessing Moral Stages: A Manual.* Mimeograph. Harvard U. Press, 1976.

Koser, C.; Lyonnet, S.; Tambuttino, G.; Matanic, A.; Lozano, J.; Scarvaglieri, G.; Valle, I.; Goffi, T.; Bombin, L. *Autorità e obbedienza nella vita religiosa.* Milan: Ancora, 1978.

LaPlace, J. (S.J.) Educating to Obedience. *Donum Dei.* (A publication of the Canadian Religious Conference), 1967, 3, pp. 43-70.

LaPotterie, I.; Pelland, G.; Spidlik, T.; Dumeige, G.; Gioia, M.; Calvez, J.Y.; Rahner, H., *Obedience—Christian, Religious, Jesuit,* Rome: Centrum Ignatianum Spiritualitatis, 1980.

Loevinger, J. Origins of Conscience. In M.M. Gill, P.S. Holzman, (Eds.) *Psychology vs. Metapsychology. Psychoanalytic Es-*

says in Memory of George Klein. New York: International Universities Press. Psychological Issues, Vol. IX, no. 14, Monograph 36, 1976, pp. 265-297.

Lonergan, B.F. (S.J.) *L'intelligenza: Studio sulla comprensione dell'-esperienza*. Alba: Edizioni Paoline, 1961.

Lozano, J.M. (C.M.F.) *Discipleship. Toward an Understanding of Religious Life*. Chicago: Claret Center for Resources in Spirituality. Religious Life Series, 1980.

Mahoney, J. Obedience: Consent or Conformity? In *The Way. Supplement*. May, 1968, pp. 5-19.

McChesney, D. To Heal the Eye of the Heart. In *The Way. Supplement*. no. 23, Autumn, 1974, pp. 3-17.

Meissner, W.W. (S.J.) The Psychology of Obedience. In *The Assault of Authority: Dialogue or Dilemma?* Maryknoll, N.Y.: Orbis Books, 1971, pp. 205-236.

Merton, T. (O.C.S.O.) *Life and Holiness*. Garden City, N.Y.: Doubleday and Co., 1963.

————. *Love and Living*, New York: Ferrar-Straus-Giroux, 1979.

————. *Seeds of Contemplation*. Norfolk, Conn.: New Directions, 1949.

Metz, J.B. *Followers of Christ. The Religious Life in the Church*. Paramus, N.J.: Paulist Press, 1978 (in particular: pp. 63-72).

————. *Poverty of Spirit*. Paramus, N.J.: Paulist Press, 1968.

Murphy, L. (S.J.) Psychological Problems of Christian Choice. In *The Way. Supplement*. no. 24, Spring, 1976, pp. 26-35.

————. Authority and Freedom. In *The Way. Supplement*. 1979, 36, Summer, pp. 71-81.

Nugent, Donald. Justice, Love and Peace. *The Way*. 19, 4, 1979, pp. 283-291.

Nuttin, J. *Psychoanalysis and Personality*. New York: New American Library, 1962.

O'Connor, J. (O.P.) Authority and Community. In *Supplement to Doctrine and Life*. Vol. 11, 1973, pp. 15-30.

Owens, J. Value and Person in Aquinas. In *Tommaso d'Aquino nel suo settimo centenario. Atti del Congresso Internazionale.* Naples: Edizioni Domenicane Italiane, 1974.

Paul VI, *La gioia Cristiana*. Rome: Vatican Typoglot Press, 1978.

Poltawski, A. Ethical Action in Consciousness. In Tymieniecka, A.T. (Ed.) *Analecta Husserliana*. Vol. VII The Human Being in Action. Dordrecht: Holland: D. Reidel, 1978, pp. 115-150.

Plé, A. (O.P.) *Obedience and Religious Life*. London: Blackfriars, 1953, pp. 130-139.

Rahner, K. (S.J.) Reflections on Obedience. A Basic Ignatian Concept. In *Cross Currents*. 1960.

_____. *The Christian Commitment. Essays in Pastoral Theology.* New York: Sheed and Ward, 1963 (In particular Chapters II, III).

_____. The Christian Teacher: Freedom and Constraint. In *Mission and Grace*. Vol. II. London: Stagbooks, 1964, pp. 116-145.

_____. Cristo modello dell'obbedienza dei sacerdoti. In *Discepoli di Cristo*. Rome: Ed. Paoline, 1968, pp. 179-180.

_____. Theology of Freedom. In *Theological Investigations*. Vol. VI. New York: Seabury Press, 1969.

_____. *Meditations on Priestly Life*. London: Sheed and Ward, 1970.

_____. *Religious Obedience in the Priesthood*. New York: Sheed and Ward, 1973, (in particular, pp. 110-113).

_____. *Theological Investigations*. Vol. III. New York: Seabury Press, 1974.

_____. The Evangelical Counsels. Religious Obedience. In G.A. McCool, (Ed.) *A Rahner Reader*. New York: Seabury Press, 1975.

_____. *The Religious Life Today*. New York: Crossroad Publ. Co., 1976.

Rahner, K. (S.J.) et al. *Nuovo stile di obbedienza*. Milan: Ancora, 1969.

Rueda, B. (F.M.S.) *Eccomi, Signore. Conversazioni sull'obbedienza*. Rome: Centro Studi USMI, Milan: Ancora, 1975.

_____. *Obedience*. "Vita Evangelica" Series-No. 10, Ottawa: Canadian Religious Conference, 1977.

Rulla, L.M. (S.J.) *Depth Psychology and Vocation: A Psycho-social Perspective*. Rome: Gregorian University Press; Chicago: Loyola University Press, 1980.

_____. *Psychology and Priestly Formation: Premises For a Dialogue*. Mimeographed, 1978, pp. 1-13.

_____. Freedom and Discipline in Religious Formation: Some Anthropological Considerations. *Proceedings of the 15th National Assembly, National Conference of Vicars for Religious*. Rome: (Buffalo: U.S.A.), March 14-22, 1981, pp. 32-43.

Rulla, L.M. (S.J.), Ridick, Sr. Joyce (S.S.C.), and Imoda, F. (S.J.) *Entering and Leaving Vocation: Intrapsychic Dynamics*. Rome: Gregorian University Press; Chicago: Loyola University Press, 1976.

Schoonenberg, P. *The Faith of Our Baptism*. IV Vols. Malmberg L.C.G.: Hertogenbosch, 1955-1962.

Silhar, S. *La filosofia della liberta nel pensiero di Joseph De Finance*. Rome: Pontificia Università Gregoriana, 1977, pp. 38-47.

Stanley, D. (S.J.) *A Modern Scriptural Approach to the Spiritual Exercises*. Chicago: Loyola University Press, 1967.

Studies in the Spirituality of Jesuits. Joy and Judgment in Religious Obedience. Vol. VI, no. 3, 1974, pp. 149-150.

Suenens, Cardinal Leo Josef. Obedience and Faithfulness. In

Obedience and the Church. London: Geoffrey Chapman, 1968, pp. 190-196.

Tillard, J.M.R. (O.P.) *Davanti a Dio e per il mondo.* Alba: Ed. Paoline, 1975. (*Before God and for the World*).

_____. *There are Charisms and Charisms. The Religious Life.* Bruxelles: Lumen Vitae, 1977.

_____. *A Gospel Path. The Religious Life.* Bruxelles, Lumen Vitae, 1978, pp. 76-126.

Tillard, J.M.R. (O.P.), Congar, Y. (O.P.) *Il rinnovamento della vita religiosa.* Firenze: Vallecchi, 1968, pp. 391-424.

Valle, I. Persona, communità e obbedienza: problemi psicologici. In *Autorità e obbedienza nella vita religiosa.* Milan: Ancora, 1978.

Van Breemen, P. *Called by Name.* Denville, N.J.: Dimension Books; 1976, pp. 21-32, 237-239.

Van Kaam, A. (C.S.Sp.) *The Transcendent Self.* Denville, N.J.: Dimension Books, 1979, pp. 28-195.

_____. *The Vowed Life,* Denville, N.J.: Dimension Books, 1968, pp. 157-168; 212-213; 240-241; 281-284.

Vergote, A. Liberté et déterminisme au regard de la psychanalyse et de l'ontologie. In *Tommaso d'Aquino nel suo settimo centenario. Atti del Congresso Internazionale.* Naples: Edizioni Domenicane Italiane, 1974.

Vitz, P. *Psychology and Religion. The Cult of Self-Worship.* Grand Rapids: William Eerdmans, 1980.

_____. *Was Jesus Self-Actualized?* New York: Addison-Wesley, 1978, pp. 7-10.

Von Balthasar, H.U. *Vocazione.* Rome: Rogate, 1981.

Waterman, A.S. Individualism and Interdependence. In *American Psychologist.* 1981, 36, 7, pp. 762-773.

The Way. Justice. Vol. 13, July, 1973. The whole issue is on justice, pp. 171-228.

The Way. Supplement 5. Feb. 1968. The entire issue is devoted to
    obedience.

Will, G. A Pope with Authority. In *Newsweek.* 1980, June 23, p. 92.

Scriptural Texts pertinent to Obedience

a. *Obedience to God:*

Gn 12:1-4; Gn 22:1-3 & 9-12; 1 K 15:22-23; Ec 4:17; Ec 46:11-12;
Jr 7:23; Jr 42:6; Lm 3:27; Ml 1:6.
Mt 22:21; Jn 8:51; Ac 4:18-19; Ac 5:29-32; Ac 9:4-6; Heb 12:9.

b. *Obedience to God's Creation:*

Jb 26:11; Jb 37:10-13; Jb 38:10-11; Ps 103:19-20; Ps 118:89, 91;
Ps 148:7-8; Ws 19:6; Is 48:13; Jr 5:22; Ba 3:33-35; Ba 6:59-62.
Mt 8:23-27.

c. *Obedience to Parents:*

Dt 21:18-21; Pr 1:8-9; Pr 6:20-23; Pr 23:22.
Ep 6:1-3; Col 2:20.

d. *Obedience to Superiors:*

Pr 15:28; Pr. 21:28.

e. *Obedience to Ecclesiastical Superiors:*

Lv 14:1-2; Dt 17:12.
Mt 8:4; Mt 23:1-3; Lk 10:16; Heb 13:17; 1 P 5:5.

f. *Obedience to Lay Superiors:*

Mt 22:16-21; Rm 13:1-7; Ep 6:5-8; Col 3:22-24; 1 Tm 6:1-2; Tt
2:9-10; Tt 3:1; 1 P 2:13-16, 18.

g. *Obedience to Christ:*

Mt 26:39-42; Lk 2:51; Jn 4:34; Jn 6:38; Jn 14:30-31; Jn 15:10; Jn
18:11; Rm 5:19; Ph 2:8; Heb 5:8; Heb 10:5-7.